THE AUTHOR

Jagan Nath Dhamija graduated from Cambridge University in English Literature and Law, and was called to the Bar from Lincoln's Inn in 1940. During the Second World War he served in the Royal Naval Voluntary Reserve.

J. N. Dhamija belongs to the former Indian Political Service. After India's Independence, he joined the Indian Foreign Service and served as Ambassador with Jawaharlal Nehru, Lal Bahadur Shastri and Indira Gandhi. His postings included four years in Afghanistan, where between 1960 and 1964 he witnessed events which were to change the country's future; and, while in Prague, he experienced the Soviet-led invasion of Czechoslovakia in 1968. After retirement he became Chairman of the International Control Commission in Laos.

His own quest for the Eternal started when he was eighteen, when his love of solitude and lonely walks by the sea taught him contemplation and gave him awareness of the Inner World. Shree Anandamayee Ma, his great Preceptor, whom he first met in 1952, has given direction and meaning to his existence.

J. N. Dhamija is married to Devika Sarabjit Singh. They have two sons, Dinesh and Sumant – who both graduated from Cambridge University. They have three grandsons, and one grandaughter; the older Biren (20) and Darun (18) have just finished 'A' levels from Harrow.

Mr and Mrs Dhamija live in New Delhi.

A QUEST FOR THE ETERNAL

POETRY, PHYSICS AND PHILOSOPHY

J. N. Dhamija

ELEMENT

Shaftesbury, Dorset • Boston, Massachusetts
Melbourne, Victoria

First published in Great Britain in 1998 by
Element Books Limited,
Shaftesbury, Dorset SP7 8BP

Published in the USA in 1998 by
Element Books, Inc.
160 North Washington Street, Boston, MA 02114

Published in Australia in 1998 by
Element Books and distributed by
Penguin, Australia, Limited
487 Maroondah Highway, Ringwood, Victoria 3134

Cover design by Slatter-Anderson
Printed and bound in Great Britain by
Creative Print and Design (Wales), Ebbw Vale

British Library Cataloguing
in Publication data available

Library of Congress Cataloguing
in Publication data available

ISBN 1 86204 360 4

What in me is dark,
Illumine, what is low, raise and support.

John Milton, *Paradise Lost*

To

The Master, Fellows and Scholars of
Emmanuel College, Cambridge

'Emma'
My *Alma Mater*

This book redeems
the promise I made to Edward Welbourne,
my Senior Tutor, later Master of Emmanuel

CONTENTS

FOREWORD

BY PROFESSOR DEREK BREWER

MOST PEOPLE, at some time in their lives, wish to find the purpose of their existence. Most of us have to be content with a pragmatic solution, largely garnered from the views of those around us. But some are more persistent, and determine to make for themselves a more coherent, to some extent a more original, or at least more personal construction of their lives and circumstances.

Such a one is J. N. Dhamija, who has lived a long life of thought and varied action through perhaps the most remarkable period of the history of the world so far. It is not my purpose, nor have I the ability, to comment here on his intense mystical contemplation of the nature of experience, as he brings together the ancient wisdom of the East with the new scientific knowledge of the West, mingling the hard-learned lessons of Christ, the Buddha, the Hindu Upanishads, and the English poets, with the observations of such eminent scientists as Planck, Einstein, Bohr, Hawking and others. Rather, I should like to welcome his work, and sketch its context in the life of this outstanding man. His life is in itself of great historical interest, especially in relation to India and Britain, spanning the period from what now seems the far-off world of 1910 to the eve of the second millennium.

I come into the story marginally, and only very recently. J. N. Dhamija came as an undergraduate to Emmanuel College, Cambridge, of which I am a Life Fellow, and was Master 1977–90, and thus we share a devotion to the same institution, which led to our first meeting in the 1980s. Eventually my wife and I visited him and his wife in New Delhi in the spring of 1995, on our way to and from a mountain trek in Nepal, and in response to their warm invitation.

It was at a lunch, during the course of that visit, at the house of one of his oldest friends, that I first experienced the special quality of the intellectual life of these two extraordinary men and their equally remarkable wives. His friend was General Malhotra, then retired, but formerly Commander-in-Chief of the Indian Army, Governor of the Punjab, ambassador to Indonesia and much else. Both Mr Dhamija, by then a retired ambassador, and General Malhotra grew up in British India; both took part in World War II, both held high office in the government of independent India and represented their country abroad. Their experience of the world is unusually wide, and they spoke unaffectedly about various aspects of it. What struck me as unusual, and unlikely, I think, to have happened in England, was that these elegant, courteous gentlemen and their wives spoke about spiritual matters with an equal lack of affectation.

I do not think I have attended many, or indeed any, lunch-parties in England where spiritual matters have been discussed as it were casually, but at the same time seriously. We talked, for example, about Hindu mythology. The details of the conversation are not important. It was neither pious nor devotional, nor, of course, was it flippant or blasphemous. It was natural. Clearly, our Indian friends were no ordinary people, nor even ordinary Indians. Yet while remaining fully Indian, they embody something that many people can seek to achieve in the mingling of the best national traditions of thought and action, in which the spiritual element is as profound as it is unobtrusive. It is from this admixture that J. N. Dhamija's book arises. In order to introduce it further, a brief sketch of his life may be of interest, both in itself, and as a part of the long history of mutually fruitful Anglo-Indian cultural and intellectual relations.

J. N. Dhamija was probably born in 1910 – although the recorded date of his birth is 17 August 1913 – to a middle-class family in a Punjabi village called Kamalia, now in Pakistan. His parents were liberal-minded people and he felt, as he tells me, that his village 'vibrated with a sacred and spiritual atmosphere.' After studying for the matriculation, which covered a number of subjects in both the Arts and Sciences, he graduated from the D. J. Sindh College, Karachi, affiliated to Bombay University, with the degree of Bachelor of Science. He studied the Sciences rather against his will in accordance with the wishes of his father, a civil engineer who proposed the same career for his son. J. N. Dhamija says that he was a very average student, with but little aptitude for mathematics, physics and chemistry, but that from an early age a strong sense of time, duty and discipline, coupled with regular habits and high idealism – always inspired by a love of natural beauty, art and poetry – sustained him through those activities for which he then had little appetite.

During the 1920s his father was posted in Karachi Port Trust where the family lived in a beautiful house on an island called Manora, part of Karachi, with fine views of sea and sky. Here it was, he says, that his 'love of solitude and lonely walks along the sea shore taught me contemplation and gave me awareness of the inner world. I developed a firm faith in the Providence who has inscrutably guided me all my life.'

It was during these solitary walks and introspections that J. N. Dhamija began his quest for the Eternal. One cannot but be struck by the similarity with the young Wordsworth, who, in a different clime, was impelled to the same quest. That quest did not impede J. N. Dhamija's desire for education: rather the reverse. He was eager to take an M.A. in English literature, and a tolerant father enabled him to attend Forman Christian College, Lahore, so that he was able to take his M.A. from the University of Punjab. By this time he was, at least according to the record, officially 23, and in 1936 he was accepted by Emmanuel College, Cambridge, to read for Part One of the relatively new English Tripos, a two-year course. However, J. N. Dhamija's passion for learning was not so all-consuming that it prevented him from spending most of his time playing tennis, and he won his tennis blue (*i.e.* he was selected to play for the University against Oxford) in his first year.

He attracted the attention of the Senior Tutor, Edward Welbourne, a celebrated, even archetypal,

College tutor both by virtue of the vigour with which he pursued his duty of care, and by the success that attended it. Welbourne told Dhamija in his second year that he had come to Cambridge not merely to play tennis but to do some study. Consequently, for his third year he changed to Law, as a number of distinguished Emmanuel men have done. Law was a one-year Tripos, in which an undergraduate could combine the achievement of a creditable second-class degree in the lower division (II:2, which was the 'career grade' in those days) with winning another blue. In 1939 Dhamija played on Wimbledon Centre Court against Bobby Riggs, who in that year won the Championship.

J. N. Dhamija feels that he owes a great deal to the perspicacity and guidance of Edward Welbourne, who had first come up to Emmanuel before World War I, from Lincolnshire. He served in the Great War, was severely wounded in the leg, and was awarded the Military Cross. A brilliant historian whose interests and habit of lateral thinking were ahead of his time, Welbourne devoted himself to teaching, to managing the tutorial side of the College, and to the art of talking. He would call on undergraduates at any time of day for a chat (woe to the tutor who would do that now, even if he had the time) and fostered a legendary college spirit, of which the benefits endure among those who, like J. N. Dhamija, knew and appreciated him. Much could be written about him, and C. Northcote Parkinson (of *Parkinson's Law* fame, himself an Emmanuel man) did so in a delightful chapter of his *A Law unto Themselves: Twelve Portraits* (London, 1966).

Meanwhile J. N. Dhamija was 'eating his dinners' (a requirement for lawyers wishing to be called to the Bar) at Lincoln's Inn, and was called to the Bar in 1940 under the shadow of war. In response to the threat, he joined the Navy and was commissioned into the Royal Navy Volunteer Reserve. During his four years of sea-going service, J. N. Dhamija went round the Cape three times, with his rare shore-leave spent at Emmanuel. Of his war service J. N. Dhamija says no more than that he was fortunate to have been given a better opportunity to know England and her people than is given to most others.

Despite his prodigious flow of speech, almost impossible to interrupt, Edward Welbourne had the ability very shrewdly to assess the person he had been talking to, and would do so in characteristically idiosyncratic style. Thus, when the time came for J. N. Dhamija to apply for a post in the Indian Government, his tutor wrote, on 12 June 1943, two separate, complementary letters, the one informal, the other formal, to Mr Lal, the High Commissioner for India, of which copies remain in the College Archive, and from which I quote the essential parts.

In his informal letter Welbourne wrote:

> He was, as a personality, an outstanding Indian student, not entirely because of his athletic powers but because he joined to personal good looks and dignified manner, a capacity for decision in majors, and a genuine desire to understand, which called on him to take several very courageous steps.
>
> I have seen a good deal of him since he left us, and we have been very glad that he has made the College his home when he has been given a short leave. If it

> is possible for him to be given an appointment in India, I feel sure he would be found to be a devoted and profitable servant.

Those were days when faithful service was thought to be both an honour and honourable.

In his second, formal letter, Welbourne wrote:

> As an undergraduate, he was an outstanding man, for he had a strong and attractive personality, and his athletic habits and successes helped him to see much more of England, and of Europe, than is possible to most young men. It helped also, for his personal decision, that the European mentality was better studied by spending time among living men, than by overmuch attention to examinations, a decision which does his good sense and courage great credit, even though it was of necessity taken at the cost of encountering difficulties with his intellectual work which he could have avoided easily by a more direct and less educational approach.
>
> When he left us, had he asked for one, I should have given him a very strong testimonial, to the effect that as a man, he had qualities of judgment, capacities for decision, courage in life, ease in personal encounter, which made him in my opinion admirably fit for Government service, that he was of high character, a man of great self control, though of energy and ambition, whose habit is to try and understand fundamentals, whose desire it is to face the hard simplicities, rather than to pleasure himself by fluent mastery over mere verbiage. I will allow his service in the Royal Navy to speak for itself.

This last sentence was a most powerful one for Welbourne, who combined deep scepticism with passionate patriotism.

There is a pleasing subtlety in these letters, but the

combination of values expressed in them, with the further personal advice to concentrate more on study, witnesses not to inconsistency but to the complexity of that old ideal of English liberal education, combining excellences of body and mind with self-control and social ease and range. The testimonials were percipient.

With further support from Lord Porter, the famous lawyer, once an Emmanuel tennis blue, Dhamija was appointed by the Secretary of State for India to the Indian Political Service in June 1944. After serving until Independence came in 1947, he joined the Indian Foreign Service. Thereafter came a series of increasingly important posts. He was Ambassador to Afghanistan, 1960–64, to Prague, 1966–69, when he was close to the events of the 'Prague Spring' and the Russian invasion, and to The Hague, 1969–71. On retirement he was appointed Chairman, International Control Commission, in Laos.

Now in full retirement, J. N. Dhamija rises every morning at four, and regularly plays nine holes of golf, before turning with undiminished zeal to the arduous intellectual pursuit of the underlying concepts of modern physical science and ancient religions of which he has created the synthesis expressed in the present book. As a work of intense contemplation and faith, coming from such a source, it must hearten any reader.

Its subject, which might be described as a 'raid on the inexpressible', is deliberately chosen as a witness to the Eternal Verities, as being of more significance than the trivia of daily existence. Its roots are in the great tradition of Indian mysticism, supplemented by some of the profound insights of both Indian religious and English Romantic poetry. By contrast, some of J. N. Dhamija's friends have pressed him to comment on the important events of the last half-century which he has witnessed. That would indeed be valuable, though much less valuable in his eyes than the self- and history-transcending flight of this book.

But even the detailed earthly record will not be lost, for since the age of eighteen he has kept a full diary, which must surely be a unique and fascinating record of such a momentous period of history. We may hope that J. N. Dhamija's diaries will be preserved in some important archive, perhaps the Royal Commonwealth Library at Cambridge, where they could be the basis for others to know of a remarkable life, in which poetry has been the springboard for a study of the Eternal Verities.

Derek Brewer, Cambridge 1998

AUTHOR'S PREFACE

THE PRESENT WORK is a modest attempt to 'justify the ways of God to man'. It deals with the How, the Why and the Wherefore of the world – the Beginning, the Being and the End of our existence.

I had once thought to record my impressions of the Indian Political Service, especially of my assignment in Gilgit, where 'the three Empires meet', the upheavals of the partition of India, the state of the Nation before, during and after partition and my impressions of the three Prime Ministers – Jawaharlal Nehru, Lal Bahadur Shastri and Indira Gandhi – with whom I served. Later, in Prague, I was a very close witness to the Soviet-led invasion of Czechoslovakia in August 1968, and having been closely acquainted with the Soviet Ambassador and other major actors in that drama, I started writing on the subject. But I abandoned it, considering that all this was ephemeral and would end up as a footnote to history. I felt that my critical appreciation and appraisal of administration, events, men and affairs would not be in keeping with the theme and spirit of the subject matter of the present work – the Eternal Verities, a theme which is for all times and for all men.

Truth is old, yet ever new. As Thomas Carlyle put it, 'the essence of originality is not that it is new; the essence of originality is sincerity. Original man is a sincere man.' It is said that most of one's ideas originate in the minds of others. Views and quotations of others, as expressed and quoted by me, I have made my own. I have thought and felt intensely and written with sincerity and conviction behind which is the experience of a full life lived over a span of eighty years.

All along an inner urge has guided and inspired me, and I am most grateful to all those whose thoughts and ideas have helped me to sustain that inspiration.

Isaac Newton's famous words that he was standing on the shoulders of giants makes one feel conscious of one's limitations and the great debt we owe to our creative forebears. And I am just a modest aspirant, striving and struggling to seek the Truth and Reality. It has been a long search and I can hardly claim to have touched the fringe of the subject whose scope, like infinity, has no bounds. I will, however, be more than satisfied if I have been able to contribute something, howsoever insignificant, to the collective thought and wisdom of Mankind.

J. N. Dhamija New Delhi 1998

The following piece, being my reminiscences of Shree Anandamayee Ma (1896–1982), was first published in the Centenary Celebration Souvenir, Ananda Jyoti in commemoration of the 100th anniversary of the birth of my Great Preceptor who has been and continues to be the inspiration of my life.

Shree Anandamayee Ma was born on 30 April, 1896 at Kheora, a tiny village in the District of Tripura (East Bengal). Born into a modest Brahmin family, She was named Nirmala Sundari (Pure Beauty). During Her childhood Ma used to go into deep absorption. At the age of twenty-two, She manifested various spiritual traits which attracted curious attention. Thereafter Her name began to spread. Seeing Her smiling looks and blissful mood, in 1925 She was named Ma Anandamayee (Bliss-Permeated Mother).

In July, 1944 Her first Ashram was established in Calcutta. In May, 1947 Prime Minister Jawaharlal Nehru accompanied by his Deputy Prime Minister Sardar Ballabh Bhai Patel, visited Her in Dehradun. In 1961 Dr Rajendra Prasad, President of India, Dr Kuta, Ambassador for Switzerland, Mr Brohi, then Pakistan's High Commissioner, came to have Her Darshan at Delhi Ashram.

She left Her body in Dehradun on Friday, the 27th August, 1982. It was brought by road in procession to Kankhal. Immediately the Prime Minister Indira Gandhi reached there when Ma's body was given Maha Samadhi. *At this sacred place a great edifice in white marble named Samadhi Mandir has been raised where people from all over India and abroad come to seek solace and recieve Her blessings. In 1987 the Government of India brought out a postage stamp to commemorate Her memory.*

MY QUEST FOR THE ETERNAL

1. *The Tryst*

WHEN I WAS ASKED to write reminiscences of my association with Ma, I was gripped with strange thoughts and feelings. A kind of wistfulness, intense longings mixed with elation, a promise of hope and fulfilment and ever-abiding Grace dominated my being.

For inexplicable reasons, I have so far been reluctant to write on the subject. For one thing it is difficult to focus on a Colossus, far larger than life, and to do justice to its delineation. The impact and impressions of Ma are too deep and profound for the understanding and comprehension of an average mind justly to record.

Memories crowd. I cannot, in a few pages, cover my whole experience of associations with Ma, which span a period of three decades. I can, however, make a modest attempt to recapitulate and narrate very briefly some of my thoughts and feelings, incidents and impressions, which perhaps may be of interest to the close and intimate circle of Ma's devotees.

I do not know how to begin and from where to begin. My Quest for the Eternal started at my age of 18. To many a place of sanctity I travelled, and many an Ashram and shrine I visited in search of my Goal. With age came some kind of knowledge, and perhaps some wisdom. But it also brought sophistication and selectiveness which made my goal recede further.

How and where to find the Perfect One – an embodiment of knowledge and wisdom and Divine Grace which could take me across the turbulent ocean of existence, dispelling the surrounding darkness with which one gets conditioned until some kind of shock or an incident awakens one to an awareness of new life?

My search continued. I had heard about Ma. But it was only in late 1952, when I returned from my first diplomatic assignment in Australia, that I had the good fortune to meet Her in person. I was then in my late thirties. At that time, the temple complex with its hall and new buildings were yet to be built at the Delhi Ashram, and Ma was staying in the house of Shri Sen at Hanuman Road. Both my wife and I went over to have Her Darshan. Ma looked at me for some time. I was simply overwhelmed by Her presence and stood speechless.

Was it a vision or a waking dream? I wondered. Her Beauty and Her Divine Grace engulfed my being with an overpowering Love.

I knew that the great moment of my life had arrived and that I had found the One whom I had been seeking for years. In my heart of hearts I then knew that I may become Godless, but Guru-less never. For me God and Guru had become one.

It was a tryst with destiny. After meeting Her an altogether new chapter opened in my life. Intense longing, a deep desire and yearning welled up within me. I simply could not live without Her. Whenever I heard that Ma was near Delhi – in Vrindaban, in Dehradun or Kankhal

– I would drive down during the weekends to these places to have Her darshan. I remember that in 1957 Ma had once come on a visit to Modinagar for about a week or so. Modinagar is some 50km away from Delhi. Every day, soon after office hours, I would drive all the way down to Modinagar and back. This restlessness and obsession, somewhat akin to madness, continued for years. I could not help seeing Her at regular intervals. But years later, by Grace Divine, this restlessness ceased. I felt that Ma was always with me and around me. Wherever I was, I could speak to Her and seek Her guidance. This experience still continues, and although Ma left Her body in August 1982, I can feel Her presence intensely whenever I call upon Her. She simply directs, controls and guides me. In fact, my whole life revolves round Her. She is the motivation which keeps me going with my deep and intense living at my age. She is my anchor. She is my Destiny and I know that She alone will complete and fulfil my life.

2. Diksha (Initiation)

> He, verily, who knows that Supreme Brahma, becomes very Brahma. *Mundaka Upanishad – 3.2.9*

The day of 23 March 1956 was a great and memorable one in our lives. Ma invariably used to go to Vrindaban during the Holy festivities. Both my wife and I eagerly looked forward to those days. With the temple and other building complexes still to come up, Ma used to live on the left side of the main entrance to the Ashram.

On the morning of 23rd March, 1956 when both

my wife and I were standing in the front of the room within Her view, Ma asked Didi, her companion since very early days, to send for us. 'How handsome this couple looks,' Ma had remarked. 'Sundar' was the word used, Didi told me later. Ma made us sit down and asked Didi to give us 'Mantra' for our daily 'Japa'. At that time we did not know anything about 'Mantras', nor about the kind of bead strings we were required to use for our 'Japa'. Detailed instructions about the daily rituals which we were enjoined to perform faithfully were given to us by Ma through Didi. This is how we received our 'Diksha'.

It was some years later that the importance and significance of the daily 'Japa' was made clear to me by Ma. She told me that apart from telling the number of beads as enjoined by Her earlier, I should continue repeating the 'Mantra' all the time under all circumstances, during day and night.

I started this practice. I then realized that it was possible to do the 'Japa' for twenty-four hours. 'Mantra' becomes part of your breath and being. It keeps on vibrating within you even during sleep and you wake up in the morning with the same vibration and awareness.

Ma thus taught me that prayer is not a part-time ritual but a full-time awareness of Truth, the way an Indian classical singer is always aware of the constant and basic 'Shruti' of Tanbura during his performance of varying notes of his raga.

Some years later, Ma told me that it was the earnestness and the intensity with which one pursued the goal that mattered. She narrated to me the state She had been through in earlier years. For six months, She was without food and cared little about Her clothes or other necessities and routines.

It then dawned upon me that God could be realized instantly, as Ramakrishna had put it, if one were to long for Him the way a drowning man struggles for his breath. I then knew and understood Ma. I knew and understood that there can be no sliding back when one reaches the state of sublimation. The knower of Brahma becomes Brahma.

3. *The Impact and the Awakening*

Sarvam Khalvidam Brahma.[1]

> Who is she that looketh forth as the morning, fair as the moon, clear as the sun, and terrible as an army with banners? *Song of Solomon*

'Just imagine that a tree – a beautiful, strong, old beech for instance approaches you with calm steps. What would you feel? "Have I gone crazy?" you would ask yourself. "Or perhaps I am dreaming." Finally you would have to concede that you had entered a new dimension of reality of which you had hitherto been ignorant.' Thus the German novelist Melita Maschmann sums up her first impressions of Ma.[2]

During the long years of my associations with Her, I have seen Ma in various aspects, in varying moods and phases. She was a living perfection in movement and action. Sometimes one may wonder how God would walk, talk and move about in our midst. Not different from Ma, I imagine. She looked resplendent in all Her majesty – a Queenly grace combined with modesty and humility seldom seen in a human mould. And it all became Her. Ma was without ego and without desire. And without desire, there cannot be any fear or anger. She was 'Paripurna'. Although unattached, the expression of Her face would change according to Her 'Bhava' and interestingly no two photographs of Her are alike when taken on two different sittings on the same day.

Prime Minister Nehru and Indira Gandhi, Ministers, Maharajahs, Judges, high officials, industrialists, businessmen, men from all walks of life, Indian and foreign, came to see Ma and returned fulfilled. There was no high or low before Her. All were welcome. They all came and after meeting Her departed with the burden of their cares reduced and their doubts removed.

Once I asked Her, 'Ma you give "privates" to others but never to me'.

'May Bhagwan never make you seek such "privates". You do not know with what troubles and tragedies most of them are afflicted when they seek such interviews.' Ma said. And I, in fact, did not have to seek such interviews. Like some other devotees I got Her response whenever and from wherever I called on Her with devotional earnestness. She always came to my rescue in Her own way during my distress.

There was something of the Omniscient and Omnipresent about Her. She knew what was happening around and what could possibly happen in future. There are several incidents and stories when Ma, like Christ, is said to have performed miracles. At least one such miracle I have seen with my own eyes. But Ma never gave an indication or impression of Her being instrumental in such extraordinary happenings. They came naturally to Her. She would simply remark that before God everything is possible, even impossible can become possible.

A miracle is nothing but the working of a Cosmic Law yet undiscovered. It is a higher law, unknown to the common man, which in its action appears strange and miraculous. And Ma knew and understood and could operate this law. For Her, past, present and future were one, being the stream of One Consciousness. And Ma was that Supreme Consciousness whose will could become the will of the Supreme. By Her mere thought (khyal) She was capable of changing one's life and destiny.

Nothing could be concealed from Her. She knew the thoughts and minds of Her devotees, the state of their being and the stages of their 'sadhna' and communicated with them accordingly.

I once happened to be alone with Ma on the terrace of the building behind the temple at Vrindaban. I was then in my fifties. Ma looked at me (implying that I was getting old) and suddenly asked: 'When are you going to do Sadhna?' I was somewhat taken aback and replied, 'Ma I will continue to do whatever you ask me to do.'

'May I give you more Japa to do?' and then before I could reply She continued: 'All right. from tomorrow you will start meditating for full one hour. You will not be able to do so at one stretch, but keep count of the time spent during intervals till you complete one hour of meditation during the whole day.'

'How and on whom I am to concentrate during the meditation?' I asked. Ma then gave me the necessary directions.

Come what may, I had to follow Ma's instructions under all conditions and circumstances. That was some twenty-five years ago. By and by, the time of my meditation increased on its own and I do not have to keep count anymore.

Ma had Her own way of imparting instructions. She reacted in accordance with your faith and approach and the stage of your development.

Whenever I found an opportunity to be alone with Ma, I would ask Her a question. Once I found Her alone and in somewhat playful mood. This also happened on the terrace of Her apartment behind the temple at Vrindaban.

'Ma, I want to become like Buddha.' I said. Ma looked at me from head to foot and said, 'You want to become Buddha! Look at the state of your mind (Isthti).' After a pause, She simply asked me the question, 'How does the world appear to you?' These words were enough to make me think seriously, and transport me to a new dimension of Reality. All of a sudden, as if in a flash, wisdom dawned upon me and I understood the implication of Ma's words.

How do I look at the world? I asked myself, and pondered.

I could then recall the great moments of my life, few and far between, when with a sudden flash of the light of discrimination, the darkness disappears and the veil of Maya is lifted. At that moment of Truth the world as it generally appears with its conflicts and discords is not. It seems to hum with sweet music, the various notes mingling together in a harmonious whole. There is joy and peace around. All things, great and small, moving and unmoving begin to look part of the stream of Consciousness in which births and deaths are forms of perennial life-flow.

You feel kinship with the whole of human-kind. The entire Universe looks resplendent with a radiant beauty. There is balance and harmony, power and elegance. And the human heart ever beating away eternally with the cosmic rhythm.

The vastness of Eternity has no bounds. Sarvam Khalvidam Brahma.

And only the Grace of Guru can give continuity and permanence to such rare moments of sublimation.

4. The Splendour of Asia

The Beauty and the Wonder and the Power!

Ma did not give any discourses, talks or lectures. She communicated by Her mere presence. Her silence spoke to us. It was uplifting and ennobling. Sometimes a word, sometimes a touch, turn of Her eye, a gesture, a movement of Her finger (usually Her left hand index finger) was enough to convey Her thoughts and wishes which served as a command and which like the Divine will had to be obeyed.

She seemed to be the repository of all knowledge and wisdom. Though She called Herself an 'illiterate little child', She could in Her own way put wise the great Mahamandleshwars who sought Her presence.

Ma reacted according to one's approach and intelligence. 'The way you play the instrument, so will you hear,' She used to say. Accordingly, at times, words of profound wisdom, touching the sublime heights of Vedanta, flowed from Her. At such times She spoke pure poetry. Here is a vignette of Her inspiring Words:

> Standing on the sea shore of Eternity, one can watch wave after wave dashing against the rocks and break, merging into infinity. How many myriads of beings are born and die at every moment and where they go disappearing into the Unknown – into infinity. This constant flux in Nature is indicative of the fact that births and deaths do not exist. There is only One Supreme Being, the infinity within us, manifesting itself into infinite forms and from which all emanate and into which all dissolve.

In Her own way Ma developed in us the best of liberal traditions. She taught us that Humanity is one – there being no essential difference between man and man.

Her approach was always constructive. She always saw unity in diversity. She never, ever uttered an unpleasant word about any person, institution or religion. According to Her, the aim and object of all religions of any race and creed, of any denomination is to take one across the turbulent ocean of existence and bring one to the Haven of peace and bliss, of freedom and light. In other words the exercise of all spiritual endeavours, howsoever diverse, is ultimately to take one to the threshold of the Eternal.

Once Ma was asked about the Hindu view of Christianity. She replied, 'If Christianity claims a special position for itself and places itself apart, it thereby breaks up all other religions. We recognize Jesus Christ, but within the unity of all religions. He himself stands above this exclusiveness'.

Ma is one of the greatest symbols of India – a country 'most richly endowed with all the wealth, power and beauty that nature can bestow'[3] – a country of great ancient culture, of tolerance and harmony of religions, a country where the human mind developed the highest truths and thought out some of the greatest thoughts in the world. In the words of Dr A. Weintrob (Swami Vijayananda), 'no one in the world has ever expressed the highest truths in such clear and sublime language as the seers of India'. And Ma was the Greatest among the great.

Whether Ma was an Avatara, Vilasa, a Siddha, a Sakta or a great Bhakta or the Divine in its Svayam Rupa – such dialectics continue and will continue. I for one know that for me Ma *is* Perfection Incarnate, Pure Consciousness, an embodiment of Sat-Chit-Anand.

Ma's contribution to the great cultural heritage of India is immense. At present we are too near to have a correct historical perspective of Her image and impact. But in ages to come posterity will hear about Her and wonder if such a being walked this earth. Like Lord Buddha, She will ever continue to shine with sparkling brilliance as one of the brightest stars in the firmament, and after thousands of years men will look at it as the Splendour of Asia, and continue to draw inspiration with devotional wonder and awe.

PROLOGUE

The Birth of Poetry

MANY A LAND, near and far, have I travelled, and I carry the seas and mountains, the skies and the varying weather, the joy and the hum of life of those lands in the innermost recesses of my soul.

I have also seen and felt the pain, sorrows and afflictions of suffering humanity and the cross we all carry from the time of our birth to the time of our crucifixion.

And I have also seen the spirit of selfless service and sacrifice prompted by urges and aspirations of freedom and light, and have witnessed the triumph of Man over Death.

But, amidst Life and Death, Silence surrounds us all. There is Silence amidst the whisperings of the wind in forests of pines. Silence rests on the golden grandeur of snowy mountain peaks. And I have seen and felt the serenity of Silence brooding over the oceans deep and spreading beyond the skies with horizons wide.

While viewing the panorama of life and nature, one can sometimes catch, by Divine Grace, a glimpse of the Spirit Supreme, which, like Silence, pervades the heart and soul of man. And when one sings in unison with that Spirit's eternal rhythm of Beauty and Love, poetry is born.

We all have moments in life when we feel an upsurge of power and immensity within. There are moments when wave after wave of peace descends, generating an incomprehensible spirit of rhythm and beauty. There are moments which give us the feeling that a handful of dust might turn to gold; that one could transform and refashion the whole world; that, at one's bidding, the mountains might move, the seas dry up, the sun and the moon change their diurnal course.

But such moments are rare in a life. Capture these moments, translate them into expressive language, and Poetry is born – the best words flowing in their best order, with apparent ease.

There is a spark of life within us, perennial, everlasting, ever new and vital, appropriately called by Carlyle the Spark of Heavenly Fire. A spark that burns and illumines, a spark that generates, sustains and sublimates.

In that sense, every human being is a poet. And if he were only to be aware of that spark, sound the depths and immensity within, and give expression to the intensity of his feelings and upsurge of emotions in an articulate and presentable form of language, he would be writing poetry.

Poetry and Values

It is said that nothing great is achieved without a dream and a song, and poetry is both dream and song. Poetry takes one to the Source – that Ultimate which is the origin of the Universe, the cause of our being and the source of all that is good, great and beautiful.

Poetry brings awareness of the harmony, rhythm and

order with which the whole Universe vibrates, and the basic purpose of life is to vibrate with this rhythm, harmony and order in our day-to-day existence: without them there is discord, conflict and unhappiness. Very few come to realize and understand the aim and purpose of life in their own lifetime.

To my mind, life begins when conceit and the arrogance of power end. The aim and purpose of life is not merely the acquisition of wealth and property, power and position, or even of name and fame. These are pursuits of the average and common mind and, in the last analysis, a measure of mediocrity. The important thing is to broaden the bounds of knowledge and to bring refinement, grace and excellence to one's life. These come readily with hard work, self-effacement and service of mankind.

But to a truly aspiring mind even those achievements are not enough: for such, the sky is not the limit. There are worlds beyond worlds. For him, the aim and fulfilment of life is to realize himself, to feel his kinship with the whole of Creation, to come face to face with the Reality, and become free and illuminated. Thus might he lighten all the world with the light of his candle. What greater service to Humanity than this![1]

But to be able to understand life and its widest and highest implications, we need a guide, and poetry can be a very good guide.

Poetry, as Wordsworth put it, is the breath and finer spirit of all knowledge. Poetry can make us emotionally aware of the Divine Inner Light which guides, which gives grace and goodness, strength and power to our existence. That light is the basis of the human values of Truth (Satyam), Goodness (Shivam) and Beauty (Sundaram).

These values are universal. Honesty and integrity, kindness and compassion, humility and unpretentiousness, dispassion and equanimity, detachment and uncovetousness and all other virtues flow therefrom. They are the basis of law and order, sense of justice, duty, discipline and punctuality. They generate feelings of liberality, freedom and goodwill. In effect, they uplift, sustain and support our lives. They shape our destinies. To deviate from these values is to come to grief. Politics, trade, any profession, once divorced from ethics and values must eventually come to a bad end. In fact, anything not based on Truth and Justice must, sooner or later, perish. This is the inexorable law of life, relentless as the law of gravity. It governs individuals, administrations, institutions and governments. It determines, in the last analysis, the rise, the decline and the fall of nations and empires.

How does this principle work? The deterioration of a government, said Montesquieu, begins almost always with the decay of its principles. One deviation from the right principle leads, like sin, to another.[2]

And what are the right principles? As aforementioned, they must, of necessity, embody such values as truth, honesty, integrity and uniformity of justice. A fall from these principles must necessarily lead to corruption and the perpetration of injustice. There are many aspects to corruption – moral, political, administrative. Corruption may take simple forms such as nepotism or bribery.

But graft and corruption in high places, especially in government and amongst ruling hierarchies, lead to the worst forms of injustice, as eventually they hit the common man the hardest.

Injustice has far more repercussions than are commonly perceived or realized by its perpetrators, repercussions which may recoil after one, two, five, or even fifty years. And it is the coming generations who have to pay and atone for the sins of their forefathers. The revolutions of the world, in fact, are nothing but the explosions of accumulated heaps of injustices. The greater the injustice, and the longer the period of its infliction, the greater the explosion. And such explosions can be more powerful than the atom bomb. They shatter and destroy the very foundations of institutions and governments, wiping out established dynasties, governments and empires.

History affords us a good model of the working of this principle, and, by its study and application, futurologists may be able to predict with some measure of accuracy the distant future of the world and the destiny of mankind.

Let us delve deep into the realm of poetry and probe the sweet mystery of life and the strange mystery of death. How can we solve the enigma of our existence – Who am I? Where did I come from? Why do I exist? and where do I go?

We all have our day-to-day conflicts, our travails and tribulations, our loves and hates, our joys, sorrows and sufferings, our fears and hopes, our longings and aspirations. And there is a natural urge to rise above them, to cross this turbulent ocean of existence which we call life, and find a haven of abiding peace and everlasting bliss.

Knowingly or unknowingly, we are all in search of that Reality which is above and beyond the pale of our existence, above and beyond sorrows and sufferings, above and beyond life and death.

In finding that Reality, one finds everything. In Him is all attainment; He is the summit of fulfilment, rest, repose, tranquillity.

Let us, then, begin at the beginning – the Beginning, the Being and the Ending of existence, and ponder over man's life, his destiny and, finally, his fulfilment.

Chapter One

IN THE BEGINNING

ACCORDING TO the widely accepted 'Big Bang' theory, billions of years ago (12 to 15 billions, as at present reckoned by cosmologists), our Universe, with its millions of galaxies, came into being. Its total mass exploded out of a primæval point of infinite density in which time and space were merged as one. It sprang into existence as if from a vacuum or void.

This explosion marks the beginning of space and time.

The Universe, according to most cosmologists,[1] is still expanding and will continue to expand until, at a distant point in time, it will start contracting, after which its total mass will be recondensed into its original state. Maybe, like the Big Bang, there will be a Big Crunch – a state of singularity in which time will cease and space will dissolve into the Primordial Void.

What existed 'before'[2] this point of Infinite Density when it exploded into the Universe? Was there an earlier Creation which, after exploding and expanding, contracted back to this point? And what exactly is this point of Infinite Density? Is it something Eternal – without beginning and without end?

Or is the Universe itself without beginning and without end? That is, has it always been in a 'steady state'? – a theory or an idea which is near to the Buddhist concept of a 'beginningless beginning'.

In speculating upon the foregoing, we come across barriers of time and thought, as we reach a stage of singularity wherein all mathematical equations break down.

Can we then say that the Universe had a beginning which was not a beginning and will have an end without an end?

The Universe was created out of a primordial void – Shunya, or the Buddhist Sunyata – and will dissolve back into it; matter turned into energy, just as, at the time of the Big Bang, energy turned into matter. During billions of years this process may repeat itself – explode, expand, contract and dissolve. And thus the play of Creation goes on, endlessly.

'In the beginning was the Word, and the Word was with God, and the Word was God.' If we substitute Primæval Energy (Shakti) or Void for the 'Word' of St John, we come near to the Big Bang model of the Universe. It stands to reason, as Stephen Hawking, the celebrated Cambridge physicist conveyed in so many words, that the Big Bang may not be very like Genesis, but at least you can regard it as a creation, and you can invoke God as Creator.

What is the nature of Vacuum or Void as perceived by scientists?

For Newton, Void, or vacuum was but nothingness, an empty stage upon which the cosmic drama unfolds. For Einstein, empty space was a participant in the great drama, 'its geometry as important to events as is terrain in a steeplechase.'

'Nothingness contains all of being' writes the physicist

Heinz R. Pagels in his book *The Cosmic Code.* 'All of physics – everything we hope to know – is waiting in the vacuum to be discovered.'[3]

'Like the Void of Eastern mysticism, the "physical vacuum" – as it is called in the field theory – is not a state of mere nothingness, but contains the potentiality for all forms of the particle world. These forms, in turn, are not independent physical entities but merely transient manifestations of the underlying Void. As the [Buddhist] Sutra says, "Form is emptiness and emptiness is indeed form".'[4]

The relation between the virtual particles[5] and the Vacuum is an essential, dynamic relation; the Vacuum is truly a 'living Void', pulsating in endless rhythms of creation and destruction.[6]

'Pure Being and Nothing are the same,' said Hegel.[7]

According to Eastern mystics, Void (Shunya) is not emptiness. It is the Source, the Ultimate Reality, the Essence of the Whole giving birth to all forms in the phenomenal world. It is the source of Energy (Shakti) which projected the Universe.[8] It is the source of all life on this earth and of life in other worlds and worlds beyond of which we may know little at present.

Zero (in Sanskrit) is Shunya, the Primordial Void of the Eastern mystics.

Sunyata is the emptiness of all conceptual designation, because it is the essence of the Whole, which lies hidden in the centre of each individual, in the innermost depth of our consciousness, which Fa-tsang calls 'the Source'.[9]

Brahma is Prana. Brahma is Joy. Brahma is the Void.[10]

Chapter Two

THE FUNDAMENTAL FORCE

Unified Theories

CHARLES DARWIN came near to the truth when he imagined creation as a Tree of Life and all animals and all plants being represented by the branches of that Tree. He should have gone a step further and said that the Tree of Life has one root with various branches representing not only various species, animals and plants, but all created things, great and small, moving and unmoving.

Primal Power is the sap which sustains the root and branches of the Tree of Life.

Modern Science, in its quest for the Ultimate Reality of the Universe, is getting more and more metaphysical. It has entered the area of Eastern mysticism.

The scientific search for simplicity and unity started with the search for the particle which constituted the ultimate building block of matter. Once it was thought that the atom was the fundamental building block. But on entering into the sub-atomic world there does not seem to be an end to this chase – the atom is composed of protons, neutrons and electrons – and the protons and neutrons incorporate clouds of particles called mesons – and there are several sorts of mesons each composed of still smaller particles named 'quarks' by scientists.

It is like peeling an onion, layer by layer; in the end there is nothing – Void – Shunya.

The unified theories offer a solution by seeking simplicity not by discovering the ultimate building block of matter but by trying to discover a single force which underlies the basic forces – the four interactions, as they are called – which govern the behaviour of these particles.

Very briefly and simply stated, these four forces are:

1) The Gravitational Force, which acts on all matter. It holds the galaxies, stars and planets together, and determines the overall features of the Universe we live in.

2) The Electromagnetic Force. In 1864, the physicist James Clerk Maxwell established that electricity and magnetism are two aspects of the same force. This force is important in the nuclear world. It is responsible for holding atoms together. It is the chief force which governs all known phenomena on earth.

3) The Strong Nuclear Force, which builds the particles of the atom. Fusion, responsible for making the sun shine, and fission, responsible for the generation of power in atomic reactors, are aspects of this force.

4) The Weak Nuclear Force, which is responsible for the various sorts of nuclear decay which result in radioactivity.

All these forces, except Gravity, are at present under the process of a 'grand unification'.

Albert Einstein married Space to Time. It was his last dream to discover the One Fundamental Force which was behind and unified all the cosmic forces. He believed that a 'Grand Unified Theory' will touch the 'grand aim of science' – which is 'to cover the greatest number of empirical facts by logical deduction from the smallest possible number of hypotheses or axioms.'[1]

Stephen Hawking, who presently holds Newton's Chair as Lucasian Professor of Mathematics at Cambridge University, is in agreement with the general view that 'to unify the four forces in a single mathematical explanation is the greatest quest in all science.'[2] Like most theoretical physicists, Hawking believes that the secret of the most elusive of all goals lies in the very early Universe, the period within the first trillionth of a second after the beginning of the Big Bang, when the four forces were probably one. In mathematical terms, Hawking would like to know exactly what happened between 10^{-33} second and 10^{-43} seconds after the Big Bang. According to him, it is there that the ultimate answer to all questions about the Universe – life itself included – lies.[3]

According to most theoretical physicists, to get a complete understanding of the Universe, one has to reach the Source, the Primordial Cause of the Creation. To that end, one has to cross the Wall of Planck Time which is at 10^{-43} second after the Big Bang. This is a point of singularity where space and time simply disappear and all laws of cause and effect and all equations break down. And despite construction of large accelerators it is becoming evident that science will never be able to go beyond this point to enable it to reach the moment of creation. Here science ends and philosophy and metaphysics take over.

Planck's Wall is the 'Universe's ultimate' beyond

which scientists, with their hitherto traditional mathematical approach, will have to take a 'leap of faith' and principally be guided by the poetic instinct, which is centred in the All-Pervading Consciousness.

Scientific investigations, deductions and formulations of the unified theory must remain incomplete until one brings into the investigation the elements of human mind, heart and consciousness. One has to contemplate and conceive with the poet's eye the first moment of creation of the Universe and how from One Single Force all the forces were created. One day, in the very near future, science will discover the One Force behind all the cosmic and other forces; the One which is the origin is also the dissolution of the Universe – the Cause is also the Effect. To achieve this goal, the scientists will have to evolve and be guided by a new theory which combines Quantum Mechanics, General Theory of Relativity (which principally is the Theory of Gravity) and Consciousness – a theory which we may call QRC – Consciousness playing the central role.

Intuitively one can perceive as also see with the seeing Light that the Fundamental Force, the Source, the Ultimate Reality is One – One without a second. Many mystics, saints and sages, poets and prophets, who had direct experience of the Ultimate have testified to the same effect. 'My Divine Mother is none other than the Absolute. She is at the same time the One and the Many and beyond the One and the Many' says Ramakrishna.

That One appears as many and the many, in fact, are One. The One cause manifests itself in separate existences of different shapes and forms of different hues and colours. In other words, the diversified existence of being is rooted in the One and spreading forth from it.

The Fundamental Force, the Source, the Ultimate Reality, God, All-Pervading Brahma – whichever name you may choose to give it – is the self-evolving cause of the Universe. This Cosmic Life Force is the source of all life. Brahma and the Shakti – the Primæval Energy – are one. The One became all – the sun, the moon and the stars, the seas, the mountains, the rocks, the earth and ether, the clay and the clod – in fact, all matter which, on analysis, is convertible into energy[4] and finally into life, progressively developed into mind, heart and human consciousness.

The Primordial Cause, the Reality behind the Universe, has intelligence which according to Einstein is of such superiority that, compared with it, all systematic thinking and acting of human beings is an utterly insignificant reflections.[5] That supreme Intelligence encompasses our thoughts and actions. It is the All Comprehending Mind that perceives all, and in which past, present and future exist all at once. This cosmic Life Force permeates the core of all sentient and non-sentient beings. It influences, shapes and fashions the affairs and destinies of men, nations and civilisations.

There is nothing beyond the realms of possibility before that All Pervasive Omnipotent Grace.

In Him we live and move and have our being. He is Alpha and Omega, the beginning and the end. He is man's destiny and life's fulfilment. His Will is law, His shadow is death, His touch immortality.

Chapter Three

THE NATURE OF REALITY

> The One who, himself without colour, by the
> manifold application of his power
> Distributes many colours in his hidden purpose,
> And into whom, its end and its beginning,
> the whole world dissolves –
> He is God!
> May He endow us with clear intellect!
>
> Svestasvatara Upanishad 4.1[1]

THE FUNDAMENTAL FORCE which is hurling the cluster of galaxies away from one another in this expanding Universe is the same force which governs the movements of stars and planets. It makes the sun shine and the earth revolve around its axis. It is the wind and the storm. It is thunder, lightning and rain. And it is the same force which gives colours to the rainbow. It is the sapidity in water, the radiance in the moon and the sun, the pure fragrances of the earth, the soft breeze which opens the petals of the rose bud and makes the flowers of the field sway with ecstasy.

The Fundamental Force is Prana, the All Pervasive, which controls the breath and breathes life into all beings – the fount of faith and desire from which welled up air, fire, water, earth and ether, the senses and the mind.[2] It is the same force which is continually vibrating in man's body, heart and mind. It is the human heart that yearns and which can comprehend the incomprehensible, the human mind which can scale the skies and scan the Universe.

It is Truth, Beauty and Goodness (Satyam, Sundaram, Shivam). It is love, hope, fear and faith which make humanity.

The Fundamental Force, which we may call the Ultimate Reality, has an infinite number of names, as Arthur C. Clarke suggested in his book *The Nine Billion Names of God*. He is invoked as Ishwar, Allah, Lord, God, Jehovah and by as many other names in many languages of many climes and countries.

He is commonly known by His attributes. His essential nature is Being – Consciousness – Bliss Absolute (Sat – Chit – Anand). He has variously been called the Good, the Great, the Merciful, the Compassionate; Truth, Beauty and Love; Mind, Intelligence; Void, the Cosmos, the Infinitude; the Unmanifest, the Indestructible, the Formless; the Immeasurable, the Immutable, the Ineffable, the Unthinkable; the Omnipresent, the Omnipotent, the Omniscient; Divine, Deathless, All-Pervading; All-Comprehensive, Absolute, Sublime and Supreme Eternal. There is no end to such names, none of which can adequately express the nature of the Reality.

The Reality, that is God, is Perfect. Word fail to describe Him. When trying to express Him in language, He becomes limited and thus imperfect. Our limited mind cannot grasp the unlimited or comprehend the Incomprehensible. The limitlessness of God is expressed in a form close to the mathematical infinite by St Gregory: 'No matter how far our mind may have progressed in the contemplation of God, it does not attain to what He is, but to what is beneath Him.'[3]

His form cannot be perceived within the range of senses. No one perceives Him with the eye. Those who know Him through the faculty of intuition, as thus seated in their hearts, they become immortal.[4]

He is self-luminous, the One Light that gives light to all. After Him, as He shines, doth everything shine. This whole world is illuminated with His Light.[5]

One tends to become lyrical when describing God. While contemplating Him, the human mind is struck with awe and wonder. A splendour of a thousand suns blazing out together in the sky might resemble the greatness and glory of That Reality.[6]

His adoration is pure poetry. He is the One, the only One, the One without a second, unborn, imperishable, without beginning and without end, ever-present, permanent, pure, immovable, unthinkable, beyond duality, beyond the range of thought.

Shining with all sense-faculties without any senses; free from qualities enjoying qualities. Without and within all beings, immovable and also movable by reason of His subtlety; imperceptible; at hand and far away is That. Not divided amid beings and yet seated distributively; That is to be known as the supporter of beings; He devours and He generates.[7]

He is the Primordial Cause, the Ancient, the Primæval Man whence the ancient energy streamed forth. Great Lord of the worlds, of all that move and stand. The Essence, the seed and origin of all to come. The beginning, the middle and the end – Dissolution, Death and Immortality.

The All-Ruler, The Almighty, the Indestructible Lord, greater than the greatest, more minute than the minutest, subtler than the subtlest, farther than the farthest, nearer than the nearest, supporter of all, of form unimaginable, refulgent as the sun beyond darkness.[8] The Infinite God of all gods, pervading all, sustaineth the three worlds. Beginningless, supreme, eternal, called neither being nor non-being.[9] He is the Supreme Self seated in the hearts of all beings. And from Him flow memory, intelligence, wisdom, courage, prosperity, fame and their absence.

He is all in all. Everywhere He hath hands and feet; everywhere eyes, heads and mouths, all-hearing. He dwelleth in the world enveloping all.[10]

There is no end of His divine powers. Whatsoever is glorious, good, great, beautiful and mighty comes forth from the fragment of His splendour.[11]

Lofty beyond all thought, the Highest intelligence, with fragments of Himself, pervades the whole Universe as consciousness. And He remains the abode of the Eternal, abode of higher knowledge, repose of peace, nectar of immortality and is transcendental bliss itself.

I believe it was Paul Davies, the physicist, who said: 'If the Universe could create itself, it would embody the power of the Creator and we should be forced to conclude that the Universe itself is God.'

Imagine the Ocean being scattered into billions and billions of drops, every drop having the might of the

Ocean and at the same time the Ocean always remaining the same and as full as ever. This is how one should view the Creator, the Universe and all its manifestations. There is a world in a grain of sand.[12] An atom is a complete replica of the Solar System, with electrons encircling a nucleus just as planets revolve round the sun. And every sub-atomic particle is an 'Energy Dance'–a cosmic dance of Creation expressing the rhythm and unity of life. It is not only a dance of creation, but a pulsating process of creation and destruction which is the very basis of the existence of matter and finally of life.[13]

Poetry, art, architecture continue to exist after the death of an individual poet or of an artist or of the architect, but not so with the Lord of Creation – the Vital Force which is the cause and origin of the Universe and also its manifestation. The creation and the Creator are one. The Creation appears and disappears with the Creator. Dance disappears with the dancer. 'Just as a spider projects its own web and then reabsorbs it into its own body, so also the One Reality projects this varied Universe and then absorbs it back into itself.'[14]

How can one distinguish the Dance from the dancer, the Sun from its rays, the Moon from the moonlight, the Creation from the Creator, and God from His Grace?

> O chestnut tree, great rooted blossomer
> Are you the leaf, the blossom or the bole?
> O body swayed to music, O brightening glance,
> How can we know the dancer from the dance?[15]

We all are sparks of the Primæval Energy which

is the cause of Creation of the Universe and also the effect. We all possess the latent powers of That Energy. If all things are part of the 'Whole', then equally the 'Whole' is contained in all its parts. The effect exists in the cause.

> The Power that created the Universe
> Is latent in all its creation.
> A grain of sand, a simple atom
> Is mighty as the whirling winds
> As mighty as the heaving Oceans
> And mighty as the Mind of Man.

World is one. And man is the World. Man is the Universe.

Man only knows his physical limitations in the sense that there are worlds beyond worlds, which he is unable to reach or even mentally encompass and comprehend. And yet there is something in us which is All-knowing, which can fathom the Unfathomable and comprehend the Incomprehensible. It is the All-Pervading Self seated in the hearts of all, the Cosmos itself which carries within itself the secret of Silence, of Life, of Death and Immortality. There is nothing beyond it, and the triumph of man lies in discovering that Self within: therein lies the final fulfilment of all life.

There is a spiritual foundation to all mankind, says Ikeda. Our spiritual nature goes beyond the framework of Space and Time and consequently cannot be confined within the ordinary limits of existence and non-existence.[16]

Standing on the shore of Eternity, one can watch wave after wave dashing against the rocks and break, merging into Infinity. How many myriads of beings are born or die at every moment and where they go, disappearing into the Unknown – into Infinity. This constant flux in Nature is indicative of the fact that the births and deaths do not exist. There is only One Supreme Being, the Infinity within us, manifesting itself in infinite forms and from which all emanate and into which all dissolve.

The foregoing is a vignette of the inspiring words of my Great Preceptor, representing the essence of the East, where human mind developed the highest truths and thought out some of the greatest thoughts in the World.

Chapter Four

THE BIRTH OF RELIGION

SOME THOUSANDS of years ago, there were virtually no geographical and political boundaries between Central Asia and the Indian sub-continent. From Balkh to Bamian and present day India, nomads and tribes moved freely.

The first Aryans who set foot on the soil of the Indian sub-continent found the land good and the landscape beautiful; a fertile land of plenty – a land of openness and of freedom. The climate was congenial, the vagaries of weather not intolerable. And there was the background of the Himalayas standing in all their might and majesty, their snow-covered peaks almost touching heaven. Along the valley of the Ganges, amidst the beauty and sublimity of these surroundings, one could view with wonder and awe the panorama of nature, breathe in and absorb the grandeur and the glory of the All-Pervading Spirit which reigned supreme in Sacred Silence.

Amidst this serene and sublime atmosphere, the Aryans contemplated Reality, Nature and Life in all its manifestations, with all its vicissitudes, its joys and sorrows and its inevitability. From such contemplations were conceived and born the hymns of the Vedas[1] which form the basis of one of the greatest religions of the world. Life is suffering. There is sorrow, cause of sorrow, cessation of sorrow and the way that leads to the cessation of sorrow. Of these four noble truths, Buddhism was born.

Man that is born of a woman is of few days and full of trouble.[2] Temporal blessings pass like a dream, beauty fades like a flower, the longest life disappears like a flash.[3]

Henry Kissinger, at one time a brooding student of Oswald Spengler, Arnold Toynbee and Immanuel Kant wrote: 'Life is suffering. Birth involves death. Transitoriness is the fate of existence. No civilisation has yet been permanent, no longing completely fulfilled. This is necessity, the fatedness of history, the dilemma of mortality.'[4]

This world is no home. It is a wilderness – a place of pain, non-eternal. The flight to freedom, light and happiness is the basic urge of the quest for Reality, an escape from the prison walls of pain and suffering, sickness and sorrow, old age and death. By seeking and finding that Reality all pains and sorrows end. In Him no want of any kind exists; all is attainment, rest, repose, tranquillity. In finding Him immortality is attained and life is finally fulfilled.

To realize that Reality, to come face to face with Him, is the ultimate aim of one's life.

> Come unto me, all ye that labour and are heavy laden and I will give you rest.[5]

During my first visit to the Papal Internuncio on taking

up my posting to The Hague in 1969, the subject of Comparative Religions was raised. 'How do you know,' I asked the Internuncio, 'that I am not more Christian than very many of them. I go to the church, kneel down and pray. And I feel the presence of Christ and God. Unlike some Christians, I have no doubts that Christ walked on water. He healed the sick, gave sight to the blind, raised Lazarus to life. But, I cannot believe,' I added, 'that the salvation of man lies only through Christ.

'Christ was born some two thousand years ago,' I continued; 'but the world has been in existence for millions of years. How am I to understand that all those born before the birth of Christ never attained salvation?'

The Internuncio was quick to reply: 'All those souls were waiting for Christ to be born to be redeemed.'

'Surely God could not be so merciless as to make those souls wait for such a long time?' I hesitatingly asked.

Not surprisingly it was in India, years later, that I got a convincing reply, from a car mechanic named Messiah, who was distributing pamphlets on Christianity. On relating to him my dialogue with the Internuncio, he simply said, 'But Christ existed since the beginning of the world.' How profound was his simplicity! Messiah conveyed to me, in simple words, that the All-Pervading Spirit, without beginning and without end, brooding over its own Omnipresence and Omniscience, existed, exists and will continue to exist 'even unto the end of the world'.[6]

Once my Great Preceptor was asked about the

Hindu View of Christianity. The Great One replied 'If Christianity claims a special position for itself and places itself apart, it thereby breaks up all other religions. We recognize Jesus Christ, but within the unity of all religions. He himself stands above this exclusiveness.'

The aim and object of all religions of any race, creed, or denomination is to take one across the turbulent ocean of existence and bring one to the haven of peace and bliss, of freedom and light. All religions are like different rivers coming from different sources, winding through different regions, flowing into the same sea – the Sea of Bliss and Tranquillity. Ultimately, the exercise of all spiritual endeavours, however diverse, is to take one to the threshold of the Eternal.

Ideas and ideologies, rituals and ceremonies and codes of conduct may differ in accordance with the different climes and countries. But the basic aim and essence of all religions is the same – God Realization. In this sense, all religions are One.

Knowingly or unknowingly man walks this earth in quest of that Reality, that haven of peace commonly known as happiness, the source of which lies within. These are, in fact, the inner urges and aspirations of mankind. But deluded we walk, unable to find the way or perceive the goal which would free us from the self-made prison of pain and sorrow. We are running, like a musk deer mad with his own perfume, running after the musk not knowing where to find it.

But there is a Way. There is hope and fulfilment. The goal can be reached by self-knowledge, self-realization, which removes the veil of ignorance by removing the difference between 'you' and 'I'.

The Self within is the self of all. That is the moment of Truth when the One stands revealed as the many and the many as the One; when realization dawns that there is a basic oneness of the Universe and of life, that the individual is part of the One Great Life that pervades the Universe.

The precepts of any religion, or any of the spiritual exercises – prayer, worship and meditation – have little meaning unless this realization becomes part of day-to-day life.

Faster than sound is light, faster than light is man's mind. But faster than mind is the All-Pervading Spirit which, if invoked from the depth of a yearning heart, can be readily realized by one who becomes intensely aware of it.

God is nearer to you than the camel's neck, said Prophet Mohammed.

I had the privilege of knowing a great sage.[7] He was blind since his childhood. He looked and spoke like Socrates. During onc of his discourses, he said that it may be written in one's fate that one will be born rich or poor, sick or healthy, high or low, lucky or unlucky. But it is never written that any person, in any station of life, belonging to any religious denomination, any caste or creed, will not be able to realize and come face to face with the Supreme Reality in this very existence if he intensely yearns for it. This great boon is given to us all.

This is a message of hope wherein lies life's glory and its fulfilment.

Chapter Five

SCIENCE AND RELIGION

> Knowledge comes, but wisdom lingers,
> and I linger on the shore.
> Tennyson

ACCORDING TO geological observations, the Earth is estimated to be 4.5 billion years old. The first living cells – that is, life in its most primitive form, – came into being around four billion years ago, while the Earth had barely settled down after its formation.

Man is supposed to have evolved from the anthropoid ape about a million years ago. According to generally-accepted anthropological findings, the anatomical evolution of human nature was virtually completed some fifty thousand years ago. The human body and brain have since remained essentially unchanged in structure and size.[1]

I wonder if we have ever thought of, or dated, the first man who contemplated the Universe in which he was placed, or the Reality behind the mystery which surrounded him. It was in him that the seeds of Religion and Science were first sown. Man has ever since wondered about the Universe he lives in and questioned the why and wherefore of his existence. He is still seeking and searching for an answer to the riddle of life, the great mystery which surrounds his being: the bondage of flesh, the bondage of space and time and the way to freedom and fulfilment. Both Science and Metaphysics, the mind and heart of man, have been pursuing diligently the endless process of enquiry, ever broadening the bounds of thought and knowledge to probe into man's physical and spiritual world.

What is the purpose of life and the meaning of existence? What is our Goal? What is Truth and the Ultimate Reality and why is it important to realize it?

Life has no meaning if it has no purpose, no goal. Man has to conquer Nature, both external and internal, to achieve the basic aim which is freedom – physical, mental and spiritual; freedom from want, hunger, disease, old age and death. Science, Art, Religion and Philosophy have place in our lives because they can help us reach the goal, besides giving grace, beauty, joy and quality to our existence, thus making our sojourn on this earth value-based, fruitful and fulfilling.

Man has a tryst with his destiny. Evolution is still evolving. And the evolution of man is not complete till he reaches the state of perfection.

We have the testimony of mystics, saints and sages of almost all ages and traditions, that to achieve that state man must inevitably realize his identity with the True, the Good and the Beautiful – the All-Pervading, Omnipotent, Divine and Deathless, whatever name one may choose to give to the Ultimate Reality. To achieve that end, man has to make a conscious endeavour, engage in ceaseless effort, to reach the threshold of the Eternal, and ultimately to acquire the attributes of the Eternal. In other words, he has to discover himself, both physically and spiritually, and in the process become a Superman – 'a supreme being possessing the greatest power and intelligence' fulfilling many of the traditional requirements of God.[2]

Science is not the invention of scientists, but is the discovery of natural laws, hitherto undiscovered. Newton's laws of gravity and motion, as applicable to the physical world, existed before they were discovered by him. Similarly, what at one time seemed to be miracles, or seem to be miracles today, are simply the operation of Cosmic Laws yet to be discovered. The same applies to Quantum Mechanics. In the light of human Intelligence and Consciousness, the observations at the sub-atomic levels are yet to be deciphered correctly.

The Cartesian view of the Universe as a mechanical system is no longer valid. Neither the human body nor this world is a machine. We live in a pulsating, vibrant and conscious Universe which is interconnected and is a whole. In view of the changed perceptions of the Universe and the unique position therein of man, the new generation of scientists has to revise the earlier views of Francis Bacon, which Descartes shared, that the aim of Science was the domination and control of external Nature.

Modern science has to rise above and to go beyond the world of matter and high technology and, instead of discovering new devices for the invention of sophisticated weapons of mass destruction, must explore new vistas, new horizons, new worlds beyond Quantum Mechanics, beyond the bounds of thought and perception. The Time has come when Science can no longer confine itself only to discovering and formulating a set of laws to predict events up to the limits set by Werner Heisenberg's Uncertainty Principle. That would be a dead end.

Science, in its attempt to discover and realize Reality, has to go beyond the existing paradigms of Physics and take poetic instincts and divine inspiration as *guides* to formulate experience – thus justifying Einstein's perception that equations become synonymous with the Eternal Verities.[3] It is here that Science and Enlightened Religion and Philosophy meet.

Paradoxically, religion in the West since earlier times has often been a stumbling block in the path of scientific progress. It was late in the seventeenth century that a demarcation line between Western Philosophy and Science began to emerge. That line of demarcation is getting blurred again after the advent of Quantum Mechanics when scientific thoughts and concepts regarding man and his Universe have begun to assume a holistic pattern.

Galileo Galilei

It was Galileo Galilei (1564–1642) who quantified the physical world. He is considered to be the first man who attempted to bring mathematical precision to his observation of experiments. Being the foremost exponent of experimental methods among Renaissance scientists, he is known as the father of modern Science. Despite facing the Inquisition and being sentenced to house-arrest for life, Galileo remained convinced of the astronomical system first promulgated by Nicholas Copernicus (1473-1542) which causes the earth to revolve on its axis and considers the Sun to be the centre of the motion of the earth and planets: the heliocentric system, as opposed to the Aristotelian theory that the earth was the centre of the Universe, stationary, and that the Sun, the Moon, the planets and all the stars moved in circular orbit around it. His work *Two New Sciences* is the genesis of modern Physics.[4]

While Galileo is considered as the father of modern Science, Descartes is rightly considered as the father of Western Philosophy in the pre-Kantian period.[5]

René Descartes

René Descartes (1596–1650) was, primarily, a philosopher. He was also a great mathematician. One of the main characteristics of his philosophy was a close alliance between philosophical reflection and the Sciences.[6] According to him, the Universe was a Great Machine, and the material Universe, and the nature of all things in it, operated according to exact mathematical laws. It was Newton who formulated those laws, by which the Great Machine runs.

Isaac Newton

Sir Isaac Newton (1642–1727) is considered the greatest pioneer of Science. He was a philosopher as well as a mathematician and physicist. He was the first scientist to be knighted, by Queen Anne. He lived to the ripe old age of 85 and exercised great influence, not only during his own lifetime but for three centuries of succeeding generations. Even until the 20th century, scientists remained the prisoners of his thoughts and theories, and the Universe continued to be seen as a Great Machine.

Newton's great contributions to Science were the Laws of Motion and the Law of Gravity. But his gravitational law does not *explain* gravity. Newton clearly felt that a true understanding of the nature of gravity was beyond comprehension.

In his *Philosophiæ Naturalis Principia Mathematica* Newton conveyed in so many words that he had not been able to discover the cause of the properties of gravity from observable phenomena. 'It is enough that gravity does really exist and act according to the laws which we have explained and abundantly serves to account for all the motions of the celestial bodies…'[7]

Albert Einstein

It was left to Albert Einstein to explain gravity – which he did in terms of the curvature of a four-dimensional space-time. According to him, gravity is not a force like other forces, but is a consequence of the fact that space-time is not uniform, as had been previously assumed: it is curved, or 'warped', by the distribution of mass and energy in it.[8]

Twentieth-century science seems to have almost reached its summit – Albert Einstein having played by far the most important role. It may appropriately be called the Century of Enlightened Physics. It is also the century of man's destiny, when man, aided by science and high technology, has become the master of his own fate. The prospects before him are total self-annihilation or the establishment of a veritable Millennium on earth.

Chapter Six

PHYSICS AND METAPHYSICS

> God does not play dice.
>
> Albert Einstein

TWO THEORIES formulated in the first half of the 20th century, which changed the entire concept of 17th-century physics are: Max Planck's Quantum Mechanics, and Albert Einstein's Theory of Relativity (Special and General).

These two theories and their resultant impact now dominate the entire field of Physics. They have brought about a radical change in man's understanding of his Universe, both internal and external. There is completely new thinking on the old concepts of space and time, mass and energy, mind and matter, cause and effect.

Quantum Mechanics

As Professor Stephen Hawking has pointed out, Quantum Theory is undoubtedly the greatest achievement in theoretical Physics this century.[1] Max Planck, the German scientist who presented his Quantum Hypotheses in 1900, is considered to be the father of this Theory. The principle being that light, X-rays, (or any other classical waves) can be emitted or absorbed only in discrete quanta, whose energy is proportional to their frequency.[2]

Very simply stated, Quantum Mechanics is a theory of atomic phenomena. It is based upon the experiments conducted in the sub-atomic world where, incredible as it may sound, Newton's physics does not apply. As verified by repeated experiments, it involves the famous Uncertainty Principle, advanced in 1927 by Werner Heisenberg, another German scientist. It states that one can never precisely measure both the position and the velocity of a particle *at the same time*; the more accurately you can measure the one, the less accurately you can measure the other. This means that unlike the clarity and precision of Newton's laws, which are based on ordinary sense perceptions and can predict events, Quantum Mechanics predicts only probabilities. Heisenberg proved that, at the sub-atomic level, there is no such thing as the 'exact sciences'. The primary significance of the Uncertainty Principle is that at the sub-atomic level we cannot observe something without changing it. This raises the question of perception involving mind, thought and consciousness, of which the implications are profound.

In the autumn of 1927, at the fifth Solvay Congress, distinguished scientists met at Brussels, when led by Niels Bohr (from Copenhagen) it was decided that it might not ever be possible to construct a model of reality. This is known as Copenhagen Interpretation. This was the first consistent formulation of Max Planck's hypothesis which can be said to have developed into Quantum Theory.

The extraordinary importance of the Copenhagen Interpretation lies in the fact that, for the first time, scientists attempting to formulate a consistent physics were forced by their own findings to acknowledge that a complete understanding of the reality lies beyond the capabilities of rational thought.[3]

Einstein did not agree with Bohr's interpretation of Quantum Theory when a great debate ensued between the two. 'The most incomprehensible thing about the World,' Einstein wrote, 'is that it *is* comprehensible.'[4] His opposition to Bohr's interpretation was expressed in his famous epigram, 'God does not play dice.'

EPR Effect

Eight years later, in 1935, in order to disprove Bohr's interpretation that Quantum Uncertainty was absolute, Einstein, along with Boris Podolsky and Nathan Rosen, published their thought experiment in a paper entitled *Can the Quantum Mechanical Description of Physical Reality Be Considered Complete?* The thought experiment demonstrated the possibility of super-luminal (faster than light) communication – a non-existent possibility according to conventional physics. The surprising consequence of thought experiment lay in a paradox: how could a measurement of a system which has interacted with another system produce an instantaneous change in the *state* of the other system, even though the two systems were separated from each other by space-like distance? This, according to Einstein, was an entirely unacceptable state of affairs as no signal could travel faster than the speed of light.

This, very briefly and very simply, has come to be known as 'EPR' effect.

Bell's Theorem

In 1964, J. S. Bell, a physicist at the European Organisation for Nuclear Research (CERN) in Switzerland, produced a mathematical formulation which demolished the theory of Einstein, Boris Podolsky and Nathan Rosen. Bell's theorem proves, in effect, the profound truth that 'the world is either fundamentally lawless or fundamentally inseparable.'[5] In 1972, Bell's mathematical construct was confirmed by physicists John F. Clauser and Stuart Freedman by experiments at the Lawrence Berkely Laboratory. They found that the statistical predictions on which Bell had based his theorem were correct. In 1982, a research team composed of physicists Alain Aspect, Jean Dalibard and Gerard Roge at the Institute of Theoretical and Applied Optics in Paris, by adding necessary refinements, further confirmed the deductions of Bell's Theorem.

This, in effect, means that Niels Bohr's interpretation of Quantum Theory stands vindicated. Heisenberg's Uncertainty Principle is now an established fact. In the words of Professor Hawking, it 'is a fundamental, inescapable property of the world.'[6]

The foregoing is a layman's broad understanding of Quantum Theory, as gleaned from the pages of well-known physiscists and knowledgeable authors on the subject. But the answer to the basic question as to, 'What is the Truth and the Ultimate Reality behind the Universe?' still seems to elude scientists.

In formulating Quantum Theory, scientists seem to have reached the threshold of Reality without being able to grasp it. They have hit upon something they are unable to comprehend, much less describe. In the words of Gary Zukav, the most profound physicists of this century have increasingly become aware that they are confronting the ineffable.[7]

Paradoxically, Albert Einstein's attempt to disprove the Uncertainty Principle led, in course of time, to the proof that:

— faster-than-light communication, of a type beyond conventional Physics, can exist between two objects separated by space-like distance.

— There is basic oneness of the Universe. At a deep and fundamental level its 'separate parts' are connected in an intimate and immediate way. (Bell's Theorem 1964)

The implications of that Theorem, as it was reworked and refined over the following ten years, are profound. According to some physicists, it is, perhaps, the most important single work in the history of physics.[8] It demonstrated scientifically that, far below the apparent variations of space-time world of matter and energy, there lies a fundamental unity in our Universe. In other words, the Universe is one whole. The world cannot be dismembered into independently-existing 'smallest units'. Every particle of matter is interconnected. An atom cannot move without affecting the whole world. There are no such things as 'separate parts'. This explains the existence of faster-than-light communication simply because 'separate parts' of the Universe are not separate; they are connected in an intimate and immediate way.

Bell's theorem conforms to the holistic pattern of the

oneness of the Universe, of All-Pervading Unity. It would also seem to support the Big Bang Theory – according to which the entire Universe is from the outset co-related – the Creator, so to speak, has become the Creation.

David Bohm's Hypothesis

David Bohm, Professor of Physics at Birkbeck College, University of London, has a broader perception of Quantum Theory, which is compatible with Bell's Theorem. Bohm offers the idea of the Universe of 'unbroken' wholeness, of an 'implicate order'. According to him, the most fundamental level, when separate parts of the Universe are connected in an intimate and immediate way, is an *unbroken wholeness* which is, in his words, 'That-which-is'. All things, including space, time and matter are forms of 'That-which-is'.[9] The deeper substratum of Reality, the level at which 'separateness' vanishes and all things appear to be part of an unbroken whole, Bohm terms as *implicate* order. Bohm did not feel that the instantaneous co-relation between particles was due to some sort of faster-than-light signalling process. Instead, he concluded that their existence suggested a non-local level of reality beyond the quantum. That is, what we perceive as separate particles in a sub-atomic system are not really separate at all, but on a deeper level of reality are merely extensions of the same fundamental 'something'.[10] Bohm asserts that there is an order enfolded into the very process of the Universe, but that enfolded order may not be readily apparent.

David Bohm is a former protégé of Einstein, and had

shared his thoughts and interacted with Krishnamurti.[11] His ideas bring modern Physics very near to the oriental philosophies propounded and practised by the sages of yore who perceived and experienced the Ultimate Truth.

The Reality is one and only one. The diversified existence of all sentient and non-sentient beings, all things moving and unmoving, is rooted in That and spreading forth from it. This is the essence of enlightened Thought and experience which dominates the Vedantic lore. The oriental concept is well expressed by Gary Zukav in the following words:

> A vital aspect of the enlightened state is the experience of an All-Pervading unity. 'This' and 'that' no longer are separate entities. They are different *forms* of the same thing. Everything is a *manifestation*. It is not possible to answer the question 'Manifestation of *what*?' because the 'what' is that which is beyond words, beyond concept, beyond form, beyond even space and time. Everything is a manifestation of that which is. That which is, *is*. Beyond these words lies the experience of that which is.[12]

According to Sir Fred Hoyle, scientific investigation indicated that the Universe is governed by some sort of interlocking hierarchy of intelligence. He gives mathematical evidence to show that the Universe was not only designed by some sort of cosmic intelligence, but that intelligence is unfathomably old – billions of years older than the age of the known Universe.[13] Paul Davies maintains that there is a cosmic design behind the present structure of our Universe.[14]

It does not need mathematical proof or Lord Orrery's

Theorem[15] to have an awareness that there is a High Intelligence behind the conscious Universe which is ever vibrating and pulsating with timeless energy.

In a sense, Einstein's stance against Bohr is vindicated. God does *not* play dice. Our world is not governed by chance. There is an order which is enfolded into the very process of the Universe.[16] There are eternal laws which transcend the thought and mind of man. There is Beauty and Rhythm, Power and Elegance. Everything is blended in one harmonious Whole.

Although Einstein did not believe in the Biblical idea of God, he was a firm believer in the inherent order and harmony of Nature and All-Pervadingness of High Intelligence which, according to him, is 'of such superiority that, compared with it, all systematic thinking and acting of human beings is an utterly insignificant reflection.'[17]

Albert Einstein, to borrow Fritjof Capra's phraseology, was one of the greatest sages of Science. He had the vision and comprehension of a mystic though he disliked his theories being related to or influenced by mysticism.

Einstein's most awe-inspiring experience was to see and contemplate the unknown, which taught him first hand 'that what is impenetrable to us really exists, manifesting itself as the highest wisdom and the most radiant beauty...'[18]

Einstein's conception of a High Intelligence permeating the Universe went beyond the belief in some kind of mechanical reality ruling from high above. Einstein was far ahead of his time. He had broad vision and a deep perception of reality and it would, to my mind, be unfair to conclude that his philosophy is essentially Cartesian.

Although, generally speaking, 'Uncertainty Principle is the fundamental feature of the Universe we live in,' Stephen Hawking, with his wider perceptions, would seem to uphold Einstein's view when he states: 'The whole history of science has been the gradual realization that events do not happen in an arbitrary manner, but they reflect certain underlying order which may or may not be divinely inspired.'[19]

With this background understanding and perception of reality, one can, intuitively, feel that Einstein was right when he said 'God does not play dice.' Conceivably he only needs to have added that in the sub-atomic world, God has gone graphic, and it needs His Intelligence to decipher His designs.

Chapter Seven

MIND, THOUGHT AND MAYA

> —We are such stuff
> As dreams are made on, and our little life
> Is rounded with a sleep.
>
> Shakespeare – *The Tempest*

HOW TO DECIPHER the Grand Design? Where does Physics go from the point of Uncertainty Principle? Will a complete understanding of the Reality behind the Universe – a life-long dream of Einstein as of other scientists – always elude science? Having reached the threshold of the Ultimate, science has yet to peer behind the veil which hides Reality. It has yet to knock at the door of the Ultimate before it opens and reveals the secrets of the Universe and of life. But, in the process, one wonders whether science will remain science, as we know it.

The sub-atomic realm is beyond the limits of sensory perception. It is also beyond the limits of rational understanding.[1] Science deals only with measurable phenomena. It cannot, like religion or poetry, comprehend the wider experience of things beyond measure. How then can it discover or describe scientifically the Reality which is beyond perception and above and beyond the thought and mind of man?

In order to probe into the 'sub-atomic realms of invisible Universe,'[2] science has to take a leap of faith, and enter the world of spirit. Even then Reality can only be experienced; it may not be described or formulated into an equation. The moment Science takes the leap of faith and enters the world of Spirit, Physics, as we know it, ceases to be Physics – it becomes Metaphysics.

Hawking states that Quantum Theory is essentially a theory of what we do not know and cannot predict.[3] According to this theory, you cannot observe something without changing it. It is essentially a theory of perception. The world does not exist independently of an observer, an entity in its own right, as Newton and other classical physicists would have us believe. It is as one observes it. It vanishes with the disappearance of the observer.

We live in a Cosmos of Consciousness which is ever vibrating with timeless energy. Since comprehension of Reality behind the Universe depends on the perception of the observer, it would seem that the proper study of the Universe and Reality behind it lies in the study of Man – his Mind, Thought and Consciousness.

Mind

The human mind is a cordless instrument which can survey the entire Universe and communicate with it. It is by far the most powerful and sensitive human organ. It is greater than all other senses. In fact, it is the basis without which the five human instruments of perception cannot function. We actually see by mind, we hear by mind, we taste, touch and smell by mind.

The human mind is one of the greatest wonders of

the world. It controls all our actions. It has a power more penetrating than X-rays. It can scale the skies, stride the stars, fathom the unfathomable. In a split second, it can not only survey the whole world but the entire Universe with its galaxies of suns and stars. And, amazingly, the human mind can study and scan itself. In the words of Alan Dresser, one of America's most brilliant young scientists, 'the marvellous thing is not the spectacle of the heavens, but the human mind which can discover, understand and contemplate the Universe.'[4]

The power of mind is limitless. The great physicist and astronomer, Sir Arthur Eddington declared 'the stuff of the Universe is mind stuff.' Thought is the measure of the Universe.[5] It can project worlds beyond worlds, giving shape and forms to 'airy nothing', and transform dreams into living reality. Imagination has no bounds. Mind can hear the whisperings of the trees with soft breeze playing in a far-off forest of pines. It can pick up distant sounds of warbling brooks and hear the twitter of birds amongst the cluster of trees. It can even hear the grass grow, perceive the delicate unfolding of the rosebuds and smell the scented aroma of the freshly rain-covered earth in the distant climes.

With power of concentration one can do and achieve what ordinarily appears miracles to a common man. A pure and balanced mind, properly developed and directed, attuned to the Eternal Fount, is capable of moving mountains. It can bring about a veritable revolution and change the complexion of the entire world.

A pure and balanced person is in control of himself. According to Swami Vivekananda, all minds are the same, different parts of one Mind. He who knows one lump of clay has known all the clay in the Universe. He who knows and controls his own mind, knows the secret of every mind, and has power over every mind.[6]

Just as we all share the same Universe, we all share the same Mind-scape.[7] Human Mind is part of the Master Mind which is Omniscient and Omnipresent. If properly attuned to that Super Satellite, it could communicate with any human mind anywhere in the world. And it is not beyond the ingenuity of science to so train an individual mind as to enable it to make such contacts on selected wave lengths and project the same, not vaguely, but as one views scenes on a television screen. That would be an improved version of telepathy. To the Master Mind, past, future and present exist as one. A human mind attuned to the Master Mind could know the secret of creation, of life and our being. It could visualize the past, present and future, of individuals, nations and civilizations.

Watch your own mind with great diligence. It is the seat of intellect, knowledge and wisdom. It is the cause of your bondage as of your liberation. It is the secret of success as also the cause of failure. It is a measure of pleasure as also of pain. Indeed, mind can make Heaven of Hell and Hell of Heaven.

The emotional aspect of one's being, commonly called the heart, is no more than the emotional phase of mind generally associated with feelings such as love and hate, rancour and compassion, mercy and forgiveness.

Thought alone preserves the sanctity of temples, mosques and churches. Thought alone transforms and deifies the idols. We create our own gods, and infuse them with the spirit of our hopes and aspirations. Thus, temples, mosques, churches and cathedrals are not mere brick and stone. Thousands of devotees have visited these sacred places, worshipped and prayed. Their thoughts and vibrations linger which infuse the atmosphere with divinity, and add grandeur and sublimity to the Houses of God.

The age of miracles is not over. Miracles abound in our world of thought and consciousness:

> At the touch of Her Grace,
> I have seen the gods become alive,
> They walk, they talk, they comfort,
> They take you to heights sublime.

Thought

Thought is the projected vibration of mind and intellect. It is, so to say, a ripple on the surface of a lake. When the mind is quiet it reflects, like still waters, the Reality beneath. Thought and mind are synonymous.

Thought is faster than sound. Sound travels in air at a speed of 1090 feet per second or 700 miles per hour. But our super-jets have overtaken the barrier of sound.

Light is faster than sound – the fastest thing known in the Universe. Light travels at a speed of 186,282 miles per second. According to experiments conducted in 1887 by two American physicists, Albert Michelson and Edward Morley, the speed of light is always constant, regardless of the motion of the observer. Physics has not been able to beat the barrier of light. And science, it seems, does not hold any hope of ever being able to overtake a flash of light in this world. However fast we go, light must still go away from us at 186,282 miles per second.[8]

Light has been proved to be both particle and wave. By virtue of its being particle, it is affected by gravity. That is why light cannot escape Black Holes[9] because of their strong gravitational pull. According to Einstein's famous equation $E=mc^2$ (where E stands for energy, m for mass and c for the speed of light), mass and energy are interchangeable. Mathematically, it would seem that light could also be converted into energy or matter, and vice versa. And it may be that one day science will invent a reactor capable of doing so – which would help to explain the seeming miracle, well known in the Indian Yogic world, of a person dematerializing in one place, and materializing in another. Rudy Rucker has recorded a series of ancient miracle-tales about Pythagoras, such as stories that he was once seen in widely separated places at the same time.[10] It might also provide an explanation for the seeming-miracle of Christ walking on the water.

The following story of an episode in the life of Lord Buddha, as narrated by L. Adams Beck, may help explain the point:

> With his great discipline and his Enlightenment, Lord Buddha had acquired super-normal powers, but he did not like to use them. But there is a record that once in the city of Rajagriha (the capital of King Bimbisara), he bade his mighty disciple Kassapa to make such a display. Immediately Kassapa, composing himself into ecstasy, was raised up in the air.

The wise know that there are no miracles, only a higher law which is unknown to the ignorant, and in its operation appears to the ignorant as strange and miraculous. Therefore did Gautama teach, that for those who have reached the higher consciousness, the bonds of time, space and form exist no more.[11] Miracles, in fact, are no more than the operation of cosmic laws, as yet undiscovered. At one time, for example, aeroplanes, the breaking of the sound barrier, jet propulsion, long-distance contact by radio, and space travel would have been thought to be miracles, but are no longer deemed so, for the laws which govern them have now been discovered.

We are all bits of the sun; we have the self-same renewing energy, which could be developed to the point where an individual becomes a superhuman reactor, capable of doing things which, ordinarily, would seem miraculous.

Almost the whole of Physics rests upon the assumption that nothing in the Universe can travel faster than the speed of light.[12] But thought certainly travels faster than light, though its speed so far has not been scientifically determined or an equation formulated.

The issue as to whether thought is a wave or a particle form – or both or neither – needs investigation. Thought is not affected by gravity. It can make a probe into a Black Hole without being trapped by its field of gravity. Einstein's equation $E=mc^2$, according to which mass and energy are interchangeable, was instrumental in inventing the atom bomb. An equation involving the speed of thought might result in something more unique than the harnessing of atomic energy. It might lead not only to a fuller understanding of Reality, but in the process lead us into the realm of what now may seem impossible, where miracles become common facts of life.

Thought is in time. When Mind takes an inspirational leap, and merges with the stream of Consciousness, it ceases to be thought. It has entered the realm of Timelessness, the repository of All knowledge, All truth, All bliss, which has no gradations and is beyond description. That invisible world, reached by thought, is more real than our phenomenal world.

The mind of a genius has much more of such inspirational interludes than the mind of a common man. In that state, mind becomes part of the Universal Mind, which is All-Pervading. That region of timelessness is above and beyond thought and intuition. In that state Truth is visible as Truth. The flood gates of knowledge open up, bringing complete transformation both in the observer and the world observed.

According to the Oriental concept the entire Universe is nothing but a thought-flash of pure Consciousness. In other words, the outer phenomenal world is only a shadowy projection of the Inner Reality which is True, Timeless, Eternal.

The Chinese Philosopher Tiantai (AD 538–97) and the great Japanese philosopher Nichiren Daishonin (AD 1222–82) propounded the teaching that a single thought-instant can contain the whole Universe, in a doctrine referred to as 'Three Thousand Worlds in a Single Thought'.[13]

In following the developments of Western scientific thought, one cannot escape the impression that the recent trend, amongst some of the modern scientists, has been to turn to ancient Eastern philosophies for a guide to a fuller understanding of the perception of the Reality behind the Universe.

To achieve the aim of conquering both external and internal nature, and to discover the underlying Reality, both East and West took different paths. The East looked inwards while the West looked outwards. With scientific advancement and the rapid flow of streams of knowledge, East and West now seem to be converging upon the same conclusion. According to Pascal, by means of thought man can grasp and absorb the whole Universe. And there is the celebrated statement of Sir James Jeans (1930) that the Universe begins to look more like a great thought than like a great machine.[14]

In fact, the Copenhagen Interpretation of Quantum Mechanics 'leads directly to the conclusion that the physical world itself is not.'[15] It is a deception of our mind. This view, by and large, conforms to the Vedantic concept.

The Concept of Maya

This world of light and shadows
Shadows larger than Life
Light flickers and dies
Shadows dance into the Night.

Stephen Hawking has stated that 'the Universe of Eastern mysticism is an illusion.'[16] This is not quite so. It is more akin to the sub-atomic world of Quantum Mechanics. It is and yet it is not. It is a mixture of both existence and non-existence.

The world has no absolute existence. It exists only in relation to the individual's mind and his five senses. This is called Maya in Vedantic Philosophy. Maya is not a theory. It is simple statement of facts, of what we are, and what we see around us.

Although scientists say that the Universe is not an illusion, they agree that it is not what our senses take it to be. This is what the Indian sages say: this world appears different from what it really is, and there is an underlying, changeless and eternal Reality which forms the basis of the Universe. Compared to that changeless Eternal, which forms and *is* the Universe, the perceived world of change, termed *Samsara* in Sanskrit, is like a dream – transitory and ephemeral.

Maya is often described as the power of thought that produces forms which are transient and therefore unreal as compared to the Eternal Reality. Thus, Maya is sometimes interpreted as power of producing illusions.

The human mind, aptly described as the 'sixth sense veiled in matter', by its very nature can be deceptive. Different observers, depending on their state of mind, see the same thing differently. Observations of phenomena in the sub-atomic world of Quantum Mechanics are a clear example of this principle: they differ from one observer to another.

Instances can also be given in the outer phenomenal world. During the day, for example, one can experience a mirage, the optical illusion of a sheet of water in a desert or on a hot road from the reflection of light. A scrap of white paper at some distance on the fairway of a golf course may give the impression of a golf ball. A common example is that of a coiled-up rope which may look like a snake in the dark or a lamp post which may appear as a ghost to a frightened child. This is 'illusion', a perception which fails to convey the true character of the thing perceived. With knowledge and in the light of discrimination, the illusion disappears and Reality appears.

It is correctly said that the fish cannot see the water in which it swims. It is the same with human beings living in this phenomenal world of change. As long as one is in the Maya, one does not recognize Maya. The dream is real as long as one is in the dream. In a dream, the mountains, the rivers, the sea, trees, people and places, seem real even though they are not observed by our physical senses, but by the perception of our mind and consciousness. Time, in a dream, is not clock-time. Years can be contained in a single moment. On waking, the dream disappears, and we are transported into another world of dreams, where things are perceived by our senses, and time is measured by man-made clocks. The nature of the experience which we go through in our phenomenal world is not different from the dream from which we have awakened.

> Life is real! Life is earnest!
> And the grave is not its goal;
> Dust thou art, to dust returnest,
> Was not spoken of the soul.[17]

The world, in each state of consciousness, is as real – and as earnest – as Longfellow would have us believe.

> The number of days of man at the most are an hundred years, as a drop of water of the sea are they

> esteemed and as a pebble of the sand, so are a few years as compared to eternity.[18]

The dream disappears at the moment of self-realization when the entire Universe reveals itself as the All-Pervading Reality – the One Brahma without a Second.

The concept of Maya is very important to explain away the Universe we live in. This world has no absolute existence; it only exists in relation to our minds and senses. According to the Advaita philosophy, of which Shankracharya was the great exponent, there is One, and only One, Reality. The One Eternal has become many, with different names and forms, the nature of which are transitory and ephemeral. This thought is beautifully expressed by Shelley in his well-known verses:

> The One remains, the many change and pass;
> Heaven's light forever shines, Earth's shadows fly;
> Life, like a dome of many-coloured glass,
> Stains the white radiance of Eternity,
> Until Death tramples it to fragments.[19]

Reality is one – the Creator *is* the creation. As the basis of all clay pots is clay, and the basis of all gold ornaments is gold, and the basis of all the waves of the sea is the ocean, so Reality is the basis of all things, great and small, moving and unmoving, with their different names and forms.[20]

Call Reality by any name; worship it, as you wish, in any form; seek its presence and grace in Church, Temple or Mosque; adore and glorify it, if you wish, as Truth, Beauty, Goodness, Infinitude, Pure Consciousness and Bliss.

The present trend of Western thought would seem to be coming closer to the Oriental concept according to which phenomena are perceived as being different manifestations of the same Reality. According to the theory of the Big Bang, the Creator became the Creation. Bell's Theorem, rooted in Quantum Theory, reveals the basic oneness of the Universe. It is One Whole which cannot be broken into independently existing smallest-units. Yet name and form make the world appear as a world of duality. The distinction between 'I' and 'You', 'We' and 'They' still defines our day-to-day existence. This is Maya.

'A human being,' wrote Albert Einstein, in reply to a letter from a Rabbi,

> is a part of the whole, called by us 'Universe', a part limited in Time and Space. He experiences himself, his thoughts and feelings as something separated from the rest – a kind of optical delusion of his consciousness. This delusion is a kind of prison for us, restricting us to our personal desires and to affection for a few persons nearest to us. Our task must be to free ourselves from this prison by widening our circle of compassion to embrace all living creatures and the whole nature in its beauty. Nobody is able to achieve this completely, but the striving for such an achievement is in itself a part of the liberation and a foundation for inner security.[21]

Einstein's 'optical delusion of Consciousness' is Maya. It is created by identification of the seer with the instrument of seeing which, like a crystal, assumes the colour of any object next to it. 'Maya is nothing but the egotism of the embodied soul. This egotism has covered everything like a veil. All troubles come to an end when the ego dies.'[22]

By the delusion of the pairs of opposites, sprung from attraction and repulsion, most of us with our human failings of want, desire, anger, attachment, passion and pride, fear and hate walk this earth wholly deluded.

It is said that there is nothing good or evil – only consequences. Good leads us to freedom, evil to bondage. We are all realized souls. Wisdom is enveloped by un-wisdom, thereby mortals are deluded.

How can we pierce the veil of Maya? The delusion created by the qualities of nature is very hard to pierce. One has to acquire knowledge and wisdom, and invoke the Eternal, to win freedom from this veil of ignorance.

Knowingly or unknowingly we are all proceeding to the same goal – perfection – the Primal Source from whence we came. When we deviate from the straight and narrow path, nature lashes us. God, in his infinite mercy and compassion, sometimes ends our sufferings by suffering.

In this world of duality, all of us, at one time or the other, have to face the inevitable. Besides day-to-day confrontations with right and wrong, natural sorrows, loss or pain, there are untold tragedies and sufferings, when human beings, in their helplessness, need to turn to the Ultimate for succour and solace. In such hours, in the words of Arnold J. Toynbee, 'religious beliefs are answers to questions that cannot be answered in scientific terms.'[23] At his son's death, Toynbee underwent a spiritual experience, which he recorded thirty years later. 'It felt as if the same transcendent spiritual presence, standing for love beyond my own, or my dying fellow human being's, capacity, had pulled aside, at that awful moment, the veil that ordinarily makes us unaware of God's perpetual closeness to us. God had revealed himself for an instant to give an unmistakable assurance of his mercy and forgiveness.'[24]

There are, in our lives, moments of ecstasy and elation, moments of selflessness and sacrifice, when the Cross becomes a symbol of sublimation, of a life fulfilled. These are moments of truth. One does not know at what auspicious moment – intense sorrow or intense joy, or perhaps a thought, a touch, a sight of beauty, dawn or sunset, a blossoming flower, a dew-drop on the leaf of grass, may, all of a sudden, transform the beholder's being, making the world appear in its naked beauty, radiant with wonder, power and glory.

With a sudden flash of the light of discrimination, the darkness disappears and the veil of Maya is lifted. At that moment of truth the world as it generally appears, with its conflicts and discords, *is not*. It seems to hum with sweet music, the various notes mingling together into a harmonious whole.

Day-to-day scenes and sights assume a new look. You 'stand and stare'.[25] You notice the dawn break; the birds sing; there is music in the air; the leaves rustle and the trees seem to sway in ecstasy; you see and feel the sun rise giving light and life; the moon and the stars move in rhythmic motion along their appointed courses; the rivulets run into the rivers, and the rivers flow, making music of their own, and merge with the sea with a sweet commotion. You observe all this – and much more.

There is joy, peace and harmony around. All things, great and small, moving and unmoving, begin to look like parts of the stream of Consciousness, in which births and deaths are forms of the perennial life-flow. You feel kinship with the whole of humanity. The entire Universe is resplendent with a radiant beauty. There is balance and harmony, power and elegance. And the human heart ever beating away with the cosmic rhythm.

The vastness of Eternity has no bounds.

Sarvam Khalvidam Brahma.[26]

Chapter Eight

CONSCIOUSNESS AND THE COSMOS

> Salutations again and again to the Devi who, pervading the entire world, abides in the form of consciousness.
>
> Devi-Mahatmyam.[1] *Durga Saptasati v.78–80*

IN THE PREVIOUS CHAPTER the question was posed, that the key to the perception of Reality behind the Universe may lie in the study of the Observer – his mind, thought and consciousness.

Having made some observations on the thought and mind of man, it might now be appropriate to examine at some length the subject of Consciousness, which alone, to my mind, may solve the riddle of the Universe and the Reality behind it – a never ending pursuit of Science and Religion since the beginning of time.

Most scientists seem to have reached the conclusion that the key to an understanding of the Quantum phenomena lies in the study and understanding of consciousness. Consciousness plays the crucial role in the process of observation. The patterns which scientists observe in nature are intimately connected with the patterns of their own minds, their concepts, thoughts and values.[2]

This is modern physicist's version of a poetic thought expressed well over hundred years ago:

> O lady! we receive but what we give,
> And in our life alone does Nature live;
> Ours is her wedding-garment, ours her shroud![3]

Consciousness seems to be an important factor in understanding the various theories connected with Quantum Mechanics. David Bohm's conception of Implicate Order and Chew's S-Matrix Theory are cases in point. Both theories recognize that Consciousness may well be an essential aspect of the Universe that will have to be included in any future theory of physical phenomena.[4]

To my mind, Consciousness is also the basic and most important factor in formulating a complete single Grand Unified Theory, the aim of which is to discover the One Fundamental Force which unifies all the Cosmic Forces.

Consciousness also offers an explanation of such unusual phenomena and occurrences as persons and objects de-materializing in one place and materializing at another, remote viewing ability, levitation, out-of-the-body experiences, clairvoyance, occultism, poltergeists, the conjuring up of disembodied spirits, and other para-normal capabilities of mind and thought. Consciousness is also the key to the study and interpretation of the strange world of dreams.

There are more things in heaven and earth than are dreamt of in our philosophy. And this is a play of Consciousness. Consciousness alone would seem to hold the key to understanding Reality and the mysteries of life and death. It could also unlock the door to the mystery which surrounds the Universe and our being and possibly offer a valid answer to Stephen Hawking's question posed in the concluding paragraph of his celebrated book *A Brief History of Time*: 'Why it is that we and the Universe exist?'

All this is readily intelligible to the Eastern mind, where the human being is regarded, not as a body with a soul, but as a consciousness with a body. In other words, we reverse René Descartes's statement – *Cogito, ergo sum* (I think therefore I am) – and affirm 'I Am, therefore I think'.

What is Consciousness? And where is it located? These questions have been extensively discussed and debated down the ages. Considering that most of one's ideas spring from the minds of others, my views on the subject are based on my acquired knowledge, personal understanding and the experience of a lifetime.

Consciousness is without shape or form, although it can project any form or number of forms. It is neither a wave nor a particle. It cannot be weighed or measured. It is not visible. It is neither a *substance* nor a *structure,* as suggested by Michael Talbot.[5] It is All-Pervading. And by virtue of it being All-Pervading, it can be said to be faster than light and thought.

We cannot exactly describe what Consciousness is. At best, a negative answer can be given: in Vedantic terms – 'Neti, Neti.'[6] 'Not this, not this' – meaning *beyond* all this. We can, however, attempt to discuss the nature of Consciousness; its power and play in the phenomenal and spiritual world; how it works and affects all sentient and non-sentient beings.

According to the Oriental concept, the entire Universe,

ever vibrating with Prana – timeless energy – is nothing but thought-flash-projection and the play of All-Pervading Consciousness.[7]

In other words, Reality pervades the Cosmos as Consciousness and various shapes and forms are different manifestations of it.

Consciousness is the warp and the woof from which the entire Universe is woven. It is the highest Intelligence. It is the Source. It is self-evolving. It pervades all things, great and small, moving and unmoving, animate or inanimate, visible or invisible. It is in every grain of sand, in every blade of grass, in the leaf of every tree, in everything, conceivable or inconceivable. The whole Cosmos is breathing in it. Every atom, every sub-atomic particle in the Universe, is vibrating with it. It is the sum total of Existence.

Scientifically, this can be easily understood according to Einstein's famous equation $E=mc^2$ (c being the speed of light), mass is nothing but a form of energy: they are mutually convertible. Matter, which has mass and occupies space, is not inert. It is active and alive. In the last analysis, as we shall see, there is no intrinsic difference between animate and inanimate objects. At the time of Creation, energy converted into matter, as matter will convert into energy at the Big Crunch[8] – the total energy of the Universe remaining exactly zero.[9]

It was through the interplay of Energy (from the inner or outer world) that living cells are supposed to have been formed some 4 billion years ago. From those primordial cells evolved and developed Man, whose anatomical evolution was essentially complete some fifty thousand years ago.[10] Thus matter converted into energy, and energy into living cells, called life, and progressively developed into mind, heart, with *human* consciousness.

Thus, matter and consciousness can be considered as fundamentally the same. And Professor Bohm has appropriately brought this under the purview of his notion of 'Implicate Order', in which any element contains enfolded with itself the totality of the Universe – his concept of totality includes both matter and consciousness.[11]

We are timeless. The play of consciousness continues projecting new shapes and forms, new worlds, new Universes.

> Eternally the great Heart beats,
> And at each stroke a new Universe is born.[12]

Consciousness pervades the Universe and is beyond the Universe. The 'Many Worlds Hypothesis' of the Western school of thought is comprehensible to the Eastern mind. Worlds beyond worlds – Universes beyond Universes – can be compared to drops in the Ocean of Consciousness. Every projected world of the Universe is like a drop in the Ocean of Consciousness, and has the attributes of that Ocean. Consciousness is self-evolving, self-contained and whole.

The developing Western thinking, that there may be nothing in the Universe that does not possess some degree of self-awareness,[13] is in accord with Oriental thought. Human Mind is part of the Universal Consciousness and, as suggested by Nobel laureate Brian

Josephson, it is within the bounds of possibility that one part of the Universe may, under certain conditions, have knowledge of another part.[14]

René Descartes referred to Consciousness as 'thinking substance'.[15] In fact, Consciousness is High Intelligence. To quote Michael Talbot, Consciousness, like the quantum, does not possess any single and precise location at all.[16] It is like an infinite circle whose circumference is nowhere but whose centre is everywhere.

According to the Aitareya *Upanishad,* Consciousness is Brahma (Pragnanam Brahma).[17] The whole Universe is contained in Consciousness. it is 'on whom the sky, the earth and the atmosphere are woven and the mind, together with all the life-breaths' (Prana).[18] Without Consciousness this world *is not*. The dance disappears with the dancer.

Consciousness is the unseen seer.[19] It is the seeing light. It is self-effulgent. It is that by which mind and all our faculties function.

> That which is the hearing of the ear, the thought
> of the mind,
> The voice of speech, as also the breathing of the breath
> And the sight of the eye![20]

In other words, Consciousness is that which is not comprehended by the mind, but by which the mind comprehends; that which is not seen by the eye but with which the eye sees; that which is not heard by the ear but by which the ear hears. It is the same power that makes the fire burn, the wind blow, the water flow and the beings breathe.

Pure Consciousness is High Intelligence. It is the

sole creator of the Universe and pervades every part of it. It is verily Brahma, the Reality which we are seeking. It is the highest God. Remain centred in it. Pray to Him that you may always remain aware of Him. Pray to Him for Light and Freedom. All other prayers are selfish. Ordinary people, as Bernard Shaw said, do not pray; they only beg.

It is said that man is made in the image of God. It would be more accurate to say that man is the projection of Pure Consciousness. Human consciousness – including self-awareness, perception, feeling, sensation, understanding, totality of mind and much else, even the sense 'of being conscious' – is part of the Pure or Universal consciousness. Human consciousness, commonly called the individual soul, when divested of dross – that is, bereft of Ego, and thereby freed from desires and fears, with its duality of good and evil, love and hate, pleasure and pain removed – is Pure Consciousness.

According to Arnold Toynbee's belief, more Indian than Judaic, 'every living creature is a temporary splinter of ultimate reality, and is reunited with this at death.'[21]

All living creatures must, however, by their own efforts, work out their own salvation before reaching the state of reunion with the ultimate Reality at death. This would be more in keeping with Indian Thought. Paul Davies has stated that we may as well say that 'the Universe *is* a mind': a self-observing as well as self-organizing system. Our own minds can in this light be viewed as localized 'islands' of consciousness, in a sea of Mind – an idea reminiscent of the Oriental conception of mysticism...'[22]

It would be more apt to say that Universe *is* Consciousness: a self-evolving, self-observing and self-organizing system, while human beings are localized islands of consciousness in that limitless ocean of Consciousness. This would be more in accord with the Oriental concept of *Atma* and *Param-Atma*.

The age-old Hindu Vedic ritual of breaking the empty earthen pot, after taking it round the dead body before cremation, illustrates the point. This ritual signifies the ardent desire of every Hindu that like the enclosed space in the earthen pot which, after it is broken, becomes the Universal space, the human consciousness (Atma) becomes part of the Universal Consciousness (Param Atma) after dissolution of the body by freeing itself from the bondage of desires which are the cause of the phenomenal fetters of pain, sorrow, sickness, old age and death.

Pure Consciousness – the All-Pervading High Intelligence – like a crystal assumes the colour of any object. Transformed in the world of life into *Jiva* (the individualized immortal spirit), it draws around itself the senses, of which Mind is the sixth, veiled in matter. It acquires the body by seizing the senses and the mind as the wind takes fragrances from their retreat.[23] Thus *Jiva,* or individual consciousness, is an integral part of the Supreme. According to Shankracharya, the *Jiva* or the self is a part of the Supreme in the same way as space in an earthen pot is part of the universal space.[24] To change the metaphor commonly used in Vedantic texts, *Jiva* or 'self' is compared to a wave in the ocean. The wave is the same as the ocean, but with different name and form. *Nirvana Mukti,* or Salvation – the final aim and fulfilment of life of every Hindu – is to become one with the nature of the Eternal and be assimilated with the Eternal. That is, divested of name and form, wave merges into the ocean – human consciousness becoming one with Pure Consciousness. This is Yoga – union of Atama with Param-Atma.

> As the flowing rivers in the ocean
> Disappear, quitting name and form,
> So the knower, being liberated from name and form,
> Goes unto the Heavenly Person, higher than the high.[25]

Pure Consciousness, or the Supreme, is One. It does not divide and partition itself into fragments. It is seated equally in all beings – unperishing within the perishing; the same Reality with different names and forms. 'Not divided amid beings and yet seated distributively; that is to be known as the supporter of beings; He destroys and He creates.'[26]

All sentient and non-sentient beings are manifestations of Pure Consciousness. One Life permeates the whole Universe. Viewed in this light, the world is one, the Universe is one. There is no difference between man and man.

Duality, the sense of separate existence, is due to name and form – different waves in one and the same ocean. It is, as Einstein has stated, an 'optical delusion of consciousness'. In the words of Nisargadatta Maharaj, it is a reflection in a separate body of the one

Reality. In this reflection the unlimited and limited are confused and taken to be the same.[27]

To undo this confusion is to become free from the bondage of name and form. This is the main purpose of life. The essence of wisdom is to see the One in the many and many in the One. One who sees the Eternal beneath the transitory can become of the nature of the Eternal – the ultimate goal of man's Evolution. This is realization of Reality – the final fulfilment of life.

Consciousness and the Cosmos

Mind-thought, Space-time and Consciousness are interwoven. It is this inter-relationship which makes the existence of the phenomenal world as we see it, possible.

Albert Einstein irrevocably linked space to time. Without the coordinates of space and time, corporeal existence is not possible. Time means duration. Space is the background against which events take place. Thus, in space, without time, events, which are comprehended by the mind, are nonexistent. Without duration, even of a spilt second, there cannot be any experience of joy or sorrow, as one would be in a state of timelessness.

And without Consciousness there would be neither space-time nor mind-thought. The cosmos and the entire world around us, which we perceive by our senses, is contained in Consciousness. And without mind our senses cannot function. Let thought cease, and there is neither time nor space. We are then in the region of timelessness and of here and now, centred in pure Consciousness which is all perfection.

Language cannot adequately express or describe (without contradicting itself) that state of timelessness. It is like being in deep and dreamless sleep during which there is neither space nor time, neither pleasure nor pain (physical or mental), neither joy nor sorrow. It is only when one is awake, or dreaming dreams, that mind and thought come into play and the dualities of joy and sorrow, light and shade, pleasure and pain is experienced.

In a dreamless state one is resting, so to speak, in Pure Consciousness, having in fact become Consciousness itself. This dreamless state is temporary, and does not occur with one's own volition. It is a quirk of consciousness. It happens rarely, and without the knowledge or conscious effort of the witness.

Besides the three states of Consciousness – namely, waking, dreaming and deep sleep – there is the fourth plane of Consciousness, called Turya or God-Consciousness. To reach this state by conscious effort and give it permanence in one's life means Self-realization. In this timeless state all is fulfilment. One is freed from the bongage of space and time, mind and thought. One has out-soared the world of pain and sorrow, of old age and death. To reach this goal is to reach the summit of evolution which man alone can aspire for, acend to and maintain.

Man and Pure Consciousness

According to Shankracharya, it is a rare boon to be born a human being.[28] Man is the masterpiece of creation. He can think, and discriminate between right and wrong, good and evil. He can survey the past, look into the future and become the master of his fate and destiny. He can understand the nature of the Eternal and can *become* the Eternal.

Man is a unique manifestation of the Play of Consciousness. Being part and parcel of the Whole, he has within him that infinite ocean of Consciousness in which the entire Universe is contained. As a wave has the strength and power of the ocean behind it, man has the strength and power of the ocean of Consciousness which pervades the Universe and guides and controls it.

Of all sentient beings, only man can become Conscious of All-Pervasive Consciousness. He can alter a Quantum event through the mere act of observation – something beyond the scope of other creatures. It has been recorded that Albert Einstein wondered, at a seminar shortly before his death, 'if a person, such as a mouse, looks at the world, does *that* change the state of the world?'[29] His doubt was not well-founded, as, unlike dogs, rats and other animals, human intelligence understands the abstract.

Of the whole Creation, man alone has freedom of action. A tiger, for example, cannot help being ferocious, the cow cannot help being docile. It is their nature. But man can be both of the nature of the tiger and the cow.

Man can acquire self-knowledge, can aspire to seek liberation from pain and sorrow, can so train and discipline himself as to be able to exercise the Supreme Will inherent in human consciousness. It must, however, be understood that only the *perception* of an ever-changing world or changeless Reality undergoes a change. It does not affect the eternal Reality.

Man's mind is profound. Its range and depth are immeasurable. It is the mind of man which gives him an awareness of Consciousness, and helps him to contemplate the True, the Divine and the Eternal. That Eternal is Brahma, One without Second. Brahma is the fount of all knowledge. Brahma is Love, Beauty, Truth, High Intelligence and Bliss. All that is good, great, glorious and mighty is but a fragment of His splendour.

It is in the nature of Love to change man into the object of his love. To know Brahma, which is all Love, is to become Brahma. When man has reached full awareness of that state, there is no sliding back to this world of duality and death. He has gone beyond the pale of joys and sorrows, pleasure and pain. He is in this world and yet above it, ever centred in Pure Consciousness. He is like a beautiful lotus flower, which remains untainted by the turbid water of the pond in which it has its roots.

He who knows Brahma sees the One in many and many in the One. He has become illuminated, shedding light and lustre upon all around him. His Compassion, love and wisdom spread in ever widening circles, giving comfort and solace to humanity. His life is complete. He has finished his work on earth and achieved the state of immortality.

Death and Immortality

In my end is my beginning –
T. S. Eliot – *Four Quartets* – 'East Coker'

According to the Oriental concept, all things, great and small, moving and unmoving, are part of the stream of Consciousness in which birth and death are seen as forms of the perennial life-flow. Birth and death mark the beginning and ending only of events in time. In timelessness there is neither birth nor death.

Man is Consciousness with a body, not a body with consciousness. And it is the nature of the body to disintegrate sooner or later. In death, therefore, only the body dies. Life remains. Human Consciousness needs another mould for its manifestation. In the words of Nisargadatta Maharaj, it is the nature of Consciousness to survive its vehicle. Like fire, it consumes the fuel, but not itself. Just as fire can outlast a mountain of fuel, so does Consciousness survive innumerable bodies. Fuel does affect the flame but only so long as the fuel lasts. When the nature of the fuel changes, the colour and appearance of the flame will change.[30]

Unlike the body, which is finite, Consciousness is infinite, immeasurable, deathless and eternal. Being indestructible, 'weapons cleave It not, nor fire burneth It, nor waters wet It, nor wind drieth It away.'[31]

Bodily existence can also be described as a state of mind, a movement in Consciousness. Birth and Death are mere ideas. Birth is merely the idea 'I am the body'; and death 'I have lost my body'. With death, the idea 'I am this body' dies; the witness does not.[32]

According to the Hindu view, birth and death are only the beginning and ending of the cycle of life. Desire is the cause of re-birth. Individual consciousness, limited as it is by the bounds of individual wants, unfulfilled desires, dreams and aspirations, needs and takes another form for its fulfilment. The manifestation of Consciousness in another body is called re-birth. It is human consciousness which goes through the 'experience' of childhood, youth, old age and then takes to a new body.[33] Thus re-birth is nothing but the materialisation of the quintessence and substance of one's past. It is the re-clothing of human consciousness with new attire.

Just as the scent of a flower comes and goes, so do our births and deaths. A new-born babe is the essence of consciousness. The child is the father of the man.

In sum, death is only the habit of a body which sooner or later *must* disintegrate. But Consciousness continues. Human Consciousness, after discarding the body, takes a new form for its fulfilment. The personality, the essence, like the scent of a flower, reappears in a new form. It is rather like being transported into a realm of Quantum Mechanics. Until the 'how of it' is worked out by the scientists, the eternal questions of Death and Immortality will remain the province of metaphysics and religion. And life will continue to remain a bitter-sweet mystery where Beauty abides and Love plays a magic role, and death as 'the undiscovered country from whose bourn no traveller returns'.

What is Immortality?

Immortality is when life and death are recognized as

essential to each other as two aspects of the same thing – the obverse and reverse of the same coin.

Immortality is not to be confused with continuity, which, in any case, is not possible in this world of change. In the words of Nisargadatta Maharaj, continuity implies identity of the past, present and future. No such identity is possible, for the very means of identification fluctuate and change. Continuity, permanence, these are illusions created by memory.[34]

Immortality is the realization, based on firm conviction, that nothing is permanent, that every beginning has an end and every end has a beginning. Nothing lasts. The process of change continues perpetually in our phenomenal world.[35]

Kings and captains, sages and saints, priests and prophets, one and all, must have their end one day. But death loses all its terror when we realize that what is alive in us is immortal, that we are timeless and, therefore, deathless – without beginning and without end.

Why does man fear death?

Firstly, he assumes himself to be the body, and secondly because he does not realize the significance and purpose of death in the scheme of Providence – that change is inherent in every fleeting moment and there can be no renewal without death.

Only those fear death who have not made the best use of life, or not realized that nothing can be retained for ever by the force of attachment. In the words of Bertrand Russell,

> But in an old man who has known human joys and sorrows and has achieved whatever work it was in him to do, the fear of death is somewhat abject and ignoble. The best way to overcome it is to make your interests gradually wider and more impersonal, until bit by bit the walls of the ego recede, and your life becomes increasingly merged in the universal life.[36]

This is intimation of immortality.

Before the end came, thus spoke Lord Buddha, his voice strong in death: 'Behold now, brethren, I exhort you. Transient are all component things. They must age and dissolve. Work out your own salvation with diligence.'

Salvation means to conquer desire and fear, sorrow and death and achieve the state of Immortality. The only way to achieve this state is to know Reality. There is no other way. After seeing the Supreme, the bonds of ego, of name and form exist no more. You are liberated for ever.

As all of a sudden the darkness of a room disappears by the light of a candle, similarly, on perceiving the Light of all Lights, the darkness of ages past is lifted.

> *Om Mani Padme Hum*, the sunrise comes!
> The dewdrop slips into the shining sea![37]

Chapter Nine

ON CONSCIOUSNESS

> You say I am repeating
> Something I have said before.
> I shall say it again.
>
> T. S. Eliot – *Four Quartets* – 'East Coker'

Consciousness and Prana

ACCORDING to the Oriental concept, Self-evolving Consciousness is the cause of the Universe. It is High Intelligence. It is the Supreme Will. Though formless, Consciousness can manifest itself in any form – gross, subtle or Supreme. It can project itself into mountains, trees, seas, stars, animals, humans – that is, the entire world of sentient and non-sentient beings.

We live, move and have our being in Consciousness. The entire Universe, the projection and play of the All-Pervading Consciousness, is ever vibrating with timeless energy. This timeless energy is called Prana.

It is very difficult to understand Prana. The subject has been extensively discussed and commented upon in the Oriental scriptures and texts. I have already very briefly touched upon some of its salient aspects.

Prana, freely translated from Sanskrit, means 'vibration'. To quote Swami Vivekananda, before creation 'when there was neither aught nor naught, when darkness was covering darkness,' Prana vibrated 'without vibrations'. The sum total of all forces in the Universe, mental and physical, when resolved back into their original state, is Prana. Thus, all these forces, whether you call them gravitation or attraction or repulsion, whether expressed as heat or electricity or magnetism, are nothing but the variations of that unit energy.[1] Breath, as is commonly believed, is not Prana. It is one of the manifestations of Prana. Ever vibrating and pulsating, Prana controls the breath and breathes life into all beings.

Prana is the Primal Energy. It is the omnipresent self-manifesting force which links together the entire Universe.

> The whole world, whatever there is,
> Was created from and moves in Prana.[2]

Thus, Pure Consciousness and Prana are synonymous. Consciousness with its vibrations is Prana, or, to put it differently, both Consciousness and Prana go together in the same way as mind and thought, space and time, ocean and waves. Consciousness contains Prana. There can be no Prana without Consciousness.

The All-Pervading Consciousness, vibrating with Prana, has made the whole world kin. This is the basis of India's age-old Vedic concept of Vasudeva Kudumbakam – the whole world is one family.

> Like the spokes of the hub of a wheel
> Everything is established in Prana.[3]

Professor Bohm's notion of the Universe of 'Unbroken Wholeness' of an 'Implicate Order' is in accord with this Vedic concept. He has merely used his own words to give a new garb to the old Oriental concept that Reality is One while appearing as many, and that the diversified existence of all sentient and non-sentient beings, of all things great and small, moving and unmoving, are rooted in One and spread forth from it. In other words, there is a basic oneness and unity of life and the Ultimate Reality underlies and unifies the multiplicity of things and events.

Prana, which may be called Cosmic Energy, is a vital and inseparable link between the worlds which form the Universe. It is the cause as well as the explanation of the workings of radio and television. It is the medium which enables us to to make contact with circulating satellites. And this inseparable link can help us to establish contact with planets and innumerable galaxies of stars, with worlds beyond worlds.

$E=mc^2$ (where c stands for the speed of light and m for mass), shows that mass and energy, being mutually convertible, are intrinsically the same. As there is no break between waters of a river, similarly there is no break between matter and matter, matter and energy, or matter and mind. Also according to the Indian philosophers, matter and mind are the same, mind being a subtle form of the matter. To quote Nisargatta Maharaj 'matter and mind are not separate, they are aspects of one energy. Look at the mind as a function of matter and you have science; look at matter as the product of mind and you have religion.'[4]

It is All-Pervading Prana that explains the working of telepathy. Man's mind, which is part of Cosmic Mind, is ever vibrating with All-Pervading Prana.

According to Swami Vivekananda, the highest result of this vibration is Thought. For the Cosmic Mind, past, present and future exist as one. It is, therefore, within the realms of possibility not only to read the minds of others but to establish contacts and communicate between minds widely separated by thousands of miles. Swami Vivekananda refers to cases where the process of healing by Prana has been carried on at a distance.[5]

Prana is Brahma.[6]

The Cosmic Energy which projects the galaxies and governs the movement of stars and planets is the same energy which is vibrating in man's body and mind. By controlling Prana, which is the sum total of Cosmic Energy, one can control the Cosmic Energy itself and acquire the powers of the Creator – Brahma.[7] According to Swami Vivekananda, all manifestations of power arise from this control. The great prophets of the world had the most wonderful control of Prana which gave them tremendous will-power. They had brought their Prana to the highest state of motion, and that gave them the power to sway the world.[8]

How do we control Prana?

To control Prana is to control the Cosmic Power of the Universe. This control is acquired by knowing and realizing the Reality, which is Brahma. To know Brahma is to become the nature of Brahma, and acquire the powers of Brahma – the Creator. This is the highest form of evolution, which man alone can aspire to and attain.

Besides other disciplines and paths – such as Gnana

Yoga,[9] Bhakti Yoga[10] and Karma Yoga[11] – known to and prescribed by Oriental philosophical schools, psychic control can achieve this aim. The knowledge and control of Prana is called *Pranayam*. Patanjali, a great Indian philosopher, who flourished *c.* 1400BC, is the greatest exponent of this Science, known as Raja Yoga. His aphorisms are the highest authority on this subject.

But, before one embarks on the great voyage in search of the Omniscient and the Omnipotent, one has to be properly equipped and prepared. Stress is laid on faith, truthfulness, non-attachment, desirelessness, cleanliness of body and purity of heart and mind. A very high price has to be paid to achieve the supreme goal of life – Realization of Reality. This realization does not come easily. It is like walking on a razor's edge. Seers, mystics, saints and aspirants all over the world have dedicated their whole lives to reach that stage of enlightenment. Vairag, that is dispassion and detachment, earnestness, deep devotion and a very strong urge and intensity of longing for truth will take one to the goal.

Consciousness and the First Cause

In the beginning was the One
The Void and the Word
Brooding over Silence of its own

Ever since the dawn of his awakening, man has wondered about the Universe in which he is placed. Physics and philosophy, science and religion have never ceased to speculate about the origin and the end of the Universe.

What existed in the beginning?

In the beginning there was neither being nor non-being, neither earth nor sky, neither sun, moon or stars. There was no light and no darkness. There was no space, and the race of time had yet to run. There was neither life nor death nor immortality.

How and whence came this creation?

According to various theological texts, God created the Universe out of primordial void. Who or what is this 'God'? The word 'God' means different things to different people and has different connotations for different schools of thought. Is God a person with form, or is He formless, or is He both? Is God an abstract principle, or an idea, or an invention of the human mind? What is His nature? What are His attributes? What are His potentialities and powers? And how could He produce something out of Nothing?

On the other hand, science, with its mathematical formulations and equations and its sophisticated machinery has in its own way been probing the secrets of the Universe, its origin, its existence and its end, and speculating about the Reality behind it.

Einstein's General Theory of Relativity implies what has been proved by mathematical theorem,[12] that the Universe must have had a beginning and may possibly come to an end.

It is now generally accepted that the Universe started with a 'Big Bang' some 15 billion years ago – as reckoned by man-made time. Its mass exploded out of a primal point of infinite density in which time and space were merged as one.

This is now being confirmed by the National Aeronautics and Space Administration (NASA) Cosmic Background Explorer satellite, COBE, which has been orbiting 500 miles above the earth since the end of 1989. It is the first time that scientists have been able to peer into the past and detected cosmic clouds some 15 billion light years from earth which explain how the stars and galaxies evolved from the Big Bang that created the Cosmos. COBE has taken a snapshot of the Universe just 300,000 years after the Big Bang, the results of which were presented to astronomers at a meeting of the American Physical Society in Washington on 28 April, 1992. Stephen Hawking declared that the news is 'the discovery of the century, if not of all time'.

In 1929 the American astronomer Edwin Hubble proved that the Universe was not static, as had been previously believed, but was expanding. Hawking described this discovery as one of the great revolutions of the 20th century.

Will the Cosmos keep on expanding for ever? Or will it, after a time, begin to contract back to the primordial point, ending up in Big Crunch singularity? The answer is, that if there is enough matter in space, gravity will slow and finally reverse the expansion of the Universe, resulting in its collapse. If, on the other hand, matter is spread too thinly, the expansion of the Universe will continue unchecked for ever. But if the amount of matter is 'just right' and the Universe is at a 'critical density', the cosmos will continue to expand, but ever more slowly, until æons from now, its growth will be barely perceptible.[13]

The early Universe, suggested Alan Guth, spread very rapidly. 'Like rays the Universe was spread.'[14] That 'inflationary' rate of expansion has slowed down to the decreasing rate of today. This would perhaps be indicative of the quantity of 'dark matter' in the Universe which exercises the force of gravity to slow and finally reverse the expansion.

At present everything astronomers can see, including all the stars and galaxies, constitutes only 1% of existing matter. The other 99% of the Universe is dark, invisible. Analysis of COBE's results may perhaps shed some light on the identity of the mysterious dark matter that constitutes most of the mass of the Universe. So there is no way of telling with certainty whether the Universe will go on expanding indefinitely or will stop expanding, reverse and finally revert to the original state of singularity.

Assumption of General Theory of Relativity apart, one may say intuitively that whatever has a beginning must have an end. Only the One without beginning is without end.

According to Professor Hawking, Albert Einstein's General Theory of Relativity is a classical theory; that is, it does not incorporate the uncertainty principle. It is not a complete theory. It tells us that the Universe must have had a beginning in 'Big Bang' singularity but it does not tell how the Universe began. The answer to this question lies in the realm of Quantum Mechanics which is inextricably mixed up with Consciousness.

Quantum Mechanics is one of the greatest theories of all times. It is the converging point of both religion and science. Its operation can be discerned in the fields of both physics and metaphysics. It permeates our thoughts and actions, and affects our day-to-day life in an inexplicable way.

In Quantum Mechanics scientists have hit upon something, the full significance of which they are unable to comprehend. They are in fact confronting the Ineffable. Here scientists have reached the threshold of the Eternal, but are unable to cross it, bound as they are by their own limitations of mathematics of measurements.

Hawking's concept of 'imaginary' time, which implies imaginary space, is one of Physics's greatest contributions to the cause of science and has profound implications. An altogether new dimension has been given to science, which, confronted by Werner Heisenberg's Uncertainty Principle, had almost reached a dead end. To my mind the concept of imaginary time is not an 'intellectual' leap as Stephen Hawking would like to call it, but a leap of intuition much more authentic than the intellectual mind-stuff. Its conception, like that of Quantum Mechanics, has yet to be fully understood.

This conception, as later explained, is readily intelligible to the oriental mind, as it implies an awareness of the the Cosmic Consciousness with which the Universe vibrates. On deeper reflection it is not difficult to grasp the totality of concept which is the main aim and end of science and religion. Once the essence of Whole is perceived, our knowledge is complete. It is said that when Plato could fully perceive the Good his philosophy ended.

It is not quite understood in the world of science that Consciousness is not the creation of Big Bang much less of man-made time which along with space and matter materialized with the Great Explosion. Consciousness is All-Pervading. It was 'before' the Big Bang. It continues and it will continue 'after' the Big Crunch.

The riddle of time is solved when it is realized that man is Consciousness with a body and not, as is generally thought in the West, a body with a soul. In that sense man is timeless. To a man of Realization, past, present, and future become as one. He lives in the state of timelessness. On reflection, the realization can dawn that it is man and his mind who are in movement, and not time. Still your mind and time will cease!

Kurt Gödel (1906–78), in his Paper of 1949,[15] attempted to show that the passage of time is an illusion. The past, present and future of the Universe are just different regions of a single vast space-time. Time is *part* of space-time, but space-time is a higher reality existing outside time. In his words – 'the illusion of the passage of time arises from the confusing of the *given* with the *real*. Passage of time arises because we think of occupying different realities. In fact, we occupy only different *givens*. There is only one reality.'[16] Professor Hawking comes nearer the mark when he considers the possibility of space-time being finite, but having no boundaries and therefore no beginning. One may venture to point out that only the One without beginning is without end and, therefore, as suggested by Professor Hawking, space-time cannot be regarded as finite.

It is endless – without beginning and without end – as indeed Professor Hawking's 'imaginary' time implies.

'Imaginary' time, the concept of which lies in the timeless state of Consciousness, is in fact the 'real' time. It has no beginning and no end. It is Eternity which is nothing but dots of present moment of timelessness. The concept of 'imaginary' time neatly fits into Quantum Mechanics. In Hawking's own words, anything which is not actually forbidden by the laws of Quantum Mechanics can and will happen. And I cannot conceive of anything which is excluded by this theory. Thus, according to the 'imaginary' time which is in accord with oriental thought, there was 'before' Big Bang and there will be 'after' the Big Crunch – the All-pervasive Consciousness existing 'before', 'during' and 'after'. In other words, the Big Bang is just a phase in the great play of Creation – a beginning and ending of an event in the stream of Consciousness. In that sense the Universe is without beginning and without end. The Universe is expanding, and beyond our Universe more Universes are being created by similar Big Bangs – the self-evolving Consciousness being the creative Cause.

Fallacious questions are sometimes asked: What was 'before' the Big Bang? Why did the Big Bang occur when it did, and not earlier or later?

The answer is that in the context of man-made time, there was no 'before'. The Big Bang did not occur in space, nor did it occur in time. Both space and time materialized with the Big Bang. Similarly, the time of occurrence of the Big Bang, at present reckoned as 15 billion years ago, relates only to a point in man-made time.

There is no past, present or future for the Eternal. Imaginary time, as explained earlier, is real time. It has no beginning and no end. It is part of the Eternity in which 15 billion years have little significance.

In the words of Professor Hawking, at the Big Bang the Universe was of zero size. Zero, in Sanskrit, is Shunya, the primordial void of the Eastern mystics. This primordial void or Shunya is not emptiness, but the Ultimate Reality called Brahma or Pure Consciousness. This basic truth is emphasized by the sages of India in the famous aphorism in Aitareya Upanishad (Rig Veda): Pragnanam Brahma[17] – Consciousness is Brahma.

The Universe, having emerged from zero or Shunya, had, according to scientists, an 'inflationary' period. When 10^{-35} seconds old to 10^{-33} seconds old it expanded from zero to about the size of grapefruit. From 3 minutes old to about 300,000 years old the Universe was a fog of free-moving charged particles that light cannot penetrate. This is the plasma period, the study of which earned the Swedish theoretical physicist Hannes Olof Gosta Alfven (1908–95) the Nobel Prize for Physics which he shared with Louis Neel in 1970.

When about 300,000 years old the expanding Cosmos cools and the particles combine into atoms; the universe becomes transparent to light. The present day universe, with stars forming in galaxies, is a result of its formation from some 2 billion years old to 15 billion years old. It still continues to expand.

Energy cannot come out of or be created out of nothing. Man's mind is struck with wonder and awe at the staggering spectacle of creation and the limitless energy which streamed forth at the time of creation.

Now that science has established that the Universe was projected out of the Void from a point of Infinite Density, it is well to examine the nature of the Void and the Primal point of the Origin.

According to Indian sages, Prana, the Omnipotent Manifesting Force, is the cause and the origin of the Universe. This Cosmic energy is the sum total of all the forces in the Universe. It includes and underlies the four basic forces – four interactions – classified by scientists as Gravitational force, the Electromagnetic force and the Strong and Weak Nuclear forces. Before creation, 'when there was neither aught nor naught, when darkness was covering darkness', Prana vibrated without vibration. As earlier stated, the All-Pervading Pure Consciousness and Prana are synonymous; and the entire Universe ever vibrating with timeless energy (Prana) is nothing but thought-flash projection and play of the All-Pervading. The Big Bang could be compared to a mighty wave in the boundless and fathomless Ocean of Consciousness.

I have attempted in earlier chapters to describe Consciousness – the Reality behind the Universe. But Consciousness defies all description. It is not possible for the human mind, with its limitations, fully to comprehend the Incomprehensible – its power, its immensity, its infinitude, its sublimity, its grandeur and its glory. The Creator is revealed in His creation, a glimpse of which a poet's eye may some time catch.

> There is not the smallest orb which thou behold'st
> But in this motion like an angel sings.[18]

I cannot resist reproducing in his own words Arnold Toynbee's impression while gazing with awe at the panorama of some of the high peaks of Himalayas –

> I was overwhelmed by their beauty and their majesty, and at the same time I realized that here Nature was revealing to me something that is beyond herself. The splendour which shines through Nature is imparted to her from a source which is beyond nature and which is the ultimate reality. If there were not this invisible spiritual presence, in and beyond the visible Universe, there would be no Himalayas and no mankind either; for mankind is part of Nature, and, like non-human Nature we owe our existence to the reality that is the mysterious common source of non-human nature and our selves.[19]

It is this 'invisible spiritual presence' which gives a glow of colour and beauty to the world, and a meaning to our existence. It is the basis of Goodness, Truth and Justice. This 'Ultimate Reality' is the High Intelligence which, according to Einstein, is of such superiority, that compared with it 'all the systematic thinking and acting of human beings is an utterly insignificant reflection.' It creates, controls, preserves, sustains, directs and dissolves. It is the All-Pervading Self-evolving Consciousness – without beginning and without end. It permeates the Primal Point of Infinite Density and will continue to permeate the expanding Universe and Universes, the contemplation of which is beyond the bounds of human mind and thought. It is the Void. It is the Word. It is the Highest God which is invoked by its various names, praised and glorified in its various shapes and forms in various places of worship. It is all in all. It reigns supreme by just a fragment of His splendour.

This Universe of name and form emerged from That – a fathomless ocean of Bliss and Beatitude – and will dissolve in it.

> Satyam, Gyanam, Anantam Brahma,
> Shantam, Shivam, Sundram Brahma,
> Anand roopam, Ekam Brahma
> Ekam Eva, Advaitam Brahma.[20]

Consciousness and the Concept of Time

Time is a man-made mathematical measure between events. It is relative. At a given instant, it is different in different parts of the world. It changes from place to place, from country to country, from one segment of the earth to another. Clocks, for example, have to be reset on the same flight from Delhi to London or from London to New York.

Even months, years, and centuries differ according to the different calendars – Christian, Bikrami, Hijri.

Ever since its beginning, the Universe has been in bondage of space and time and man, by his own devices, has added to his bondage. We run our lives, as John Boslough has put it, by clocks, calendars and numbers which we ourselves have created.[21]

Besides clock time there is also psychological time, which, depending on the state of one's mind, can stop or advance the flow of time. Both psychological time and clock time are relative.

Pythagoras is the first man known to have asked: Are days and miles necessary?[22]

On the universal scale, neither places nor instants turn out to have meaning in themselves, but only when combined into events. Thus, there is really no such time as *now* except in some place, and there is no such place as *here* except at some time.[23]

The riddle of time is solved when the basic fact is realized that time is a mathematical measure invented by man, who is timeless.

According to the Oriental concept there is no such thing as 'real' or 'imaginary' time. Time is here and now – Eternity being nothing but continuous dots of present moment. And in that sense it can be said that time leads one to timelessness. One can hear the familiar echo of the Upanishads in T. S. Eliot's words:

> Only through time time is conquered.[24]
>
> Time the destroyer is time the preserver.[25]
>
> Time present and time past:
> Are both perhaps present in time future,
> And time future contained in time past.[26]

Eliot's words are easily intelligible to the oriental mind which regards man not as body with a soul but consciousness with a body. With Self-realization, past, present and future merge and man becomes timeless. Time as we know it then ceases to exist and man becomes part of the timeless stream of All-Pervading Consciousness, where the bonds of time and space and form exist no more. 'Neither time nor space exist for one who knows the Eternal.'[27]

Quisquis Deum intelligit Deus fit.[28]

Man and his position in the Universe

Man inhabits this world, which is a small satellite revolving round the sun, an average star amongst the millions of such stars and their satellites which constitute the ever-expanding Universe. But Man is not as small and insignificant as his position in the Universe would seem to signify. He has in him the aspiration and the will to reach the Ultimate and become the Ultimate. Man alone is capable of being conscious of All-Pervading Consciousness and in the process to become the centre of the Universe – Supreme, Timeless, Eternal.

Why does he feel so helpless, beset and burdened with worries, and bound by a hundred ties of expectations?

Man suffers because he lives in time, oscillating between hope and fear. In timelessness all is perfect, all is here and now. Past is memory. Future is imagination mixed with fear and hope. Both past and future are in time. Present is not in time. And the present is all that one can control and command.

Millions of years are a mere drop in the ocean of Eternity, and Eternity is in the spilt second of the *now*. Live in the present moment and the future will take care of itself. Live in the present moment and there is no past and no future. Live in the present moment and there is no desire, no fear. Live in the present and you are face to face with the Reality – timeless perfection.

Whatever has a beginning must have an end. Time cannot take us out of time as space cannot take us out of space. All you get by waiting is more waiting. Absolute perfection is here and how, not in some future, near or far.[29]

Still your mind, and simply *be*. It is you and your mind which are in movement, and not time. Stop moving and time will cease, past and present merging into the eternal now. Just as every wave subsides into the ocean, so does every moment return to its source. Realization consists in discovering the Source, and abiding there.[30]

Let us understand that our sufferings are due to our own ignorance and are of our own making. That there is nothing permanent except change; that death is not the opposite of life but an essential aspect of it. 'To perceive life and death as essential is enlightenment and total realization.'[31]

Let go. The All-Pervading, Highest Intelligence surrounds and supports you. That mysterious power which sustains the three worlds will sustain you and your small burdens. He knows what is best for you. He is holding and guiding you. Only be convinced that He is with you. Taking refuge in the Eternal is liberation.

It is beautifully said that better indeed is knowledge than constant practice; than knowledge, meditation is better; than meditation, renunciation of the fruit of action. On renunciation follows peace.[32]

Just *be*. The greatest wisdom is to discover the highest truth and to live in harmony with it. In the process nothing has to be given up. Dross will drop away on its own. And on the glimpse of the Supreme the dawn will break, ending the bondage of space and time, of fear and sorrow, of old age and death.

So wake up and live! It is a beautiful world. Live

for the sheer joy of living. So live, as to radiate joy, love and compassion all around you. So live, as to feel kinship with the whole world when your will becomes the will of the Providence and you become your own destiny.

Prayer and the Play of Consciousness

The power that created the Universe is latent in all its creation. Man being the projection of Consciousness, carries within himself the latent power and strength of that Consciousness, which is synonymous with Brahma, the Creator. He has, therefore, in him the inherent power of that Supreme Will which it is possible for him to exercise. To quote Nisargadatta Maharaj, 'not only is the entire Universe reflected in man, but also the power to control the Universe is waiting to be used.'[33]

Thus man in fact answers his own prayers. He projects his own gods and deities and infuses in them the spirit, power and attributes of his own faith. And that particular god or deity answers the prayers in accord with his faith-projected attributes. Thus, in effect, your prayers are not answered by someone apart, a deity sitting in heaven, but by your own self.

Man alone is capable of becoming conscious of Pure Consciousness. Thus, he alone can exercise his willpower which is part of the Supreme Will. The exercise of this will can be strengthened, developed and sustained by firm faith and intense prayer. Prayer or devotion is in fact nothing but sublimated Love – the basic urge and emotion behind the First Cause.

Fervent prayer is invariably answered. It cannot be otherwise. It is, as Shelley put it,

> The worship the heart lifts above
> And the Heavens reject not.
> The desire of the moth for the star,
> Of the night for the morrow,
> The devotion to something afar
> From the sphere of our sorrow.[34]

Intense prayer takes you to the Source. It can make you profoundly aware of the All-Pervading Consciousness; when one becomes part of it and develops the powers of the Creator and exercises those powers. The Supreme Will may work through nature or through individuals who are nothing but part of the same All-Pervading Consciousness of which you or the god or deity whom you project are a part.

In the words of Swami Vivekananda, Christ and Buddha are simply occasions upon which to objectify our own inner powers. It is, in fact, your own will which answers prayers, only it appears under the guise of different religious conceptions to each mind. We may call it Buddha, Jesus, Krishna, Jehovah, Allah, Agni, but it is only the Self, the 'I'.[35]

Ralph Waldo Emerson, famous for his Essays, also wrote poetry. He was well versed in the Gita and seems to have derived his inspiration from the Upanishads, whose influence is unmistakable in his works, especially his poem 'Brahma'. His thought reflects this philosophical background when he describes man as 'a god playing the fool'.

Man, in fact, is much more than that. It is not

possible to describe God, but it is possible for man to *become* Him. Man, as earlier stated, alone is capable of becoming aware of Pure Consciousness, and in the process capable of becoming and being the veritable God. Thus, man himself is his own God, his own future, his own fate, his own destiny and fulfilment.

Tat Twam Asi[36] – That Thou Art. This is one of the Vedantins *Maha Vakya* – inspired sayings uttered in a state of sublimation. It is similar to *Aham Brahma Asmi* – I am Brahma,[37] *Ayam Atma Brahma* – the Self is Brahma,[38] and *Pragnanam Brahma*–Consciousness is Brahma.[39] *Shivo Aham* – I am Shiva and similar aphorisms are all variations of the central theme of the four Vedas. This is the essence of Vedantic philosophy, which is reflected in the sublimated utterance of Christ, 'I and my Father are one.'[40]

God and the Proof of God

In the words of Henry Luce, all higher religions are rev elations of different aspects of the same Truth.[41] It is an ancient Vedic concept that 'Truth is one, sages call it by various names'.

What is Truth? Professor Bohm used the phrase 'fundamental something' to describe 'That-which-is'. It is the same as Krishnamurti's 'Insight', Paul Brunton's 'Oversoul', Nisargadatta Maharaj's 'Awareness' and the Vedantic 'Brahma' or 'Pure Consciousness'. It is High Intelligence – 'the inscrutable wisdom of the Universe' commonly called God. It is Truth – the Reality which we are seeking.

Unlike the unreal, Reality never changes or ceases to

be. It is without beginning and without end. It is imperishable. It is the same yesterday, today and for ever.

An attempt has been made earlier to describe the nature of Reality. But it is beyond description, beyond the limits of thought and understanding. It is That which is beyond name and form, beyond space, time and causation, beyond being and non-being, beyond Death and immortality.

And yet it forms the fabric of everything. Though formless, it can project varying shapes and forms – Gross, Subtle and Supreme. It is the inner essence of all sentient and non-sentient beings. It is All-Pervading. It is breath of our breath, life of our life. It is within and without. It is all and all – in this world and beyond it.

The Creator is the Creation. Like the waves in the Ocean, the Universe with its manifold manifestations, with varying names and forms, originates, exists and dissolves in it.

In the darkness of ignorance, a coiled-up rope looks like a snake, but in the light of discrimination the delusion disappears. It is the same with the world in which we live. In the light of discrimination this world is nothing but Brahma – the All-Pervading Consciousness bathed in beauty, wonder, power and all-embracing Love.

In 1984, Sir John Eccles, Nobel laureate, announced the discovery of what he believed to be biochemical evidence supporting the existence of the human soul. And Michael Talbot discourses on the mathematical evidence for the existence of God.42 We have our limitations of language, mind and thought. But a God which requires mathematical or logical proof, or can be expressed in a precise definition, is no God. The Reality that is God can only be felt and experienced and that also remotely. Although defying description it is given to man to become the Reality – the river merging into the Ocean and becoming the Ocean. We human beings are like Ramakrishna's oft-quoted salt doll trying to ascertain the taste of the Ocean and discover its depth. There is only the experience – the experience of Nothingness – Void, Infinitude, Shunya.

Silence reigns Supreme.

More Thoughts on Death

Life flows like a river between opposing banks of pleasure and pain until it reaches the limitless Ocean of Tranquillity – the supreme goal of bliss and beatitude. As there is no break in the waters of the river, so there is no break in the flow of life. There are only ripples and waves, seldom smooth, usually turbulent.

According to the Oriental concept, birth and death are seen as the beginning and the ending of events in the stream of Consciousness. It is Consciousness which assumes the new body and it is Consciousness which discards it. The delusion that man is the body is caused by an optical illusion. It is similar to the illusion caused when reflection of a person in the mirror is confused with the actual person.

Our thoughts and actions, our hopes and fears, our desires, our aims and aspirations – that is, our Karma past and present – constitute our personality which is being shaped from day to day.

Our Karmas are fed into the sub-layers of our consciousness – a Quantum-like computer which gives results Quantum-wise. These results, like our perception of the Quantum World are, at present, beyond the comprehension of human understanding and logic.

Man, being Consciousness with a body, is timeless. The results of Karmas may appear immediately – or after days, months or years, as reckoned by man-made clocks. But appear they must, unless one breaks the computer by attaining to the state of singularity, difficult to attain, when all equations, all permutations and combinations to give destined and ordained results of past and present Karmas are effaced. That state of singularity can be achieved by being attuned to the Eternal and thus acquiring the powers of the Eternal.

The computerized version of one's personality forms part of the sensitive and inexplicable world of Consciousness. What we call death is nothing but the withdrawal of consciousness from the mind and intellect of a particular body, thus ending a particular name and form. And birth is nothing but the result of computerized past, the essence of former personality with a new name and form which Consciousness has newly acquired.

Death comes because at one time or the other, for one reason or the other, in our heart of hearts we have intensely wished it so as to escape from the afflictions of body and mind, from the self-made prison of sorrows and sufferings. Even accidents can be said to be preordained as being the working of the computerized Karmas of immediate present or past, which, like our day-to-day wishes and desires, our hopes and fears, words and deeds become stored in the deeper layer of Consciousness, to give results at one time or the other. Thus, in the last analysis, every death is akin to suicide.

> We are
> Immortal Spirits! We die at our own will,
> The stars are writ on our brow, in our hands
> Directing feelings, thoughts and actions.
> Our subtle will, miscalled fate is stamped
> Upon the sub-conscious Self – a part of
> All-Pervading Consciousness – the Will Supreme.

The entire humanity, being play of the All-Pervading Consciousness, is one. Every individual is responsible for the sufferings and death of other individuals. Similarly, the sorrows and sufferings of any individual affect the whole world. With the death of an individual, part of humanity dies. This is often explained as a consequence of Original Sin which humanity ever carries like a cross.

Conclusion

Before the beginning, in the beginning, during and after the beginning was the Eternal – the All-Pervading Consciousness. This Self-evolving Cosmic Life Force projected itself as the Universe with all its galaxies of sun and stars and planets – all things great and small, moving and unmoving. The Creator became the creation manifesting itself into different shapes and forms of varying hues and colours.

This Cosmic Life Force is imbued with High Intelligence. It is Supreme. It is the source of all life, the source of power and strength, the source of beauty, harmony, balance and rhythm. It is all in all. It governs and controls the immutable laws which make the sun shine, the fire burn, the wind blow and the waters flow.

> Verily, O Gargi, at the command of that Imperishable, the sun and the moon stand apart. Verily, O Gargi, at the command of that Imperishable the earth and the sky stand apart. Verily, O Gargi, at the command of that Imperishable, the moments, the hours, the days, the nights, the fortnights, the months, the seasons, and the years stand apart. Verily, O Gargi, at the command of that Imperishable some rivers flow from the snowy mountains to the east, others to the west, in whatever direction each flows.[43]

That Supreme Intelligence, Lord and Law, is working out the mighty evolution. Our goal is freedom – physical, mental and spiritual, freedom from want, freedom from sickness, pain and sorrow, freedom from old age and death. We are timeless. Millions of years are a mere drop in the Ocean of Eternity. But, man must inevitably reach the perfect state of pure being, ending up in transcendental Bliss and Peace – the waves merging into the Ocean of Tranquillity. This process can be hastened. The Truth is hard to discover. But there is the way when you can 'hold Infinity in the palm of your hand'.[44]

We all evolved from One Source. The main aim and purpose of life is to discover and reach that Source – the All-Pervading Brahma. One who knows Brahma becomes Brahma.[45] In that state of sublimation, Time and Space do not exist; past, present and future merge into one. All things, great and small, moving and unmoving begin to be seen as part of the stream of Consciousness in which births and deaths are forms of perennial life-flow. In the state of Super

Consciousness one is released from sickness, sorrow, old age and death. Death dies because you are one with Life. Pain and sorrow end because you are one with the Absolute Bliss – of which there are no gradations.

This is man's final destiny – the summit of Evolution. It is Realization of Reality. And therein lies life's fulfilment.

Chapter Ten

THE THEORY OF RELATIVITY – I

> The final conclusion is that we know very little, and yet it is astonishing that we know so much, and still more astonishing that so little knowledge can give us so much power.
>
> Bertrand Russell *ABC of Relativity*

HAVING GIVEN some thought to Quantum Theory in the preceding pages, it is important to discuss the Theory of Relativity, the second great Pillar of 20th-century physics, and examine how far it has taken science towards the understanding and quest for the Reality behind the Universe and to what extent it has solved the question of the why and wherefore of the world.

Science is not the invention of scientists. It is the discovery of already existing Cosmic Laws. Like Newton's Law of Gravity, which he formulated on the fall of an apple, Albert Einstein's Theory of Relativity is the discovery of an already existing set of simple facts which form part of the Immutable Laws. The Theory of Relativity, like earlier scientific discoveries, helps us better to understand the Universe in which we find ourselves. The theory is important as it has altered the hitherto-held view by the physicists of the fundamental structure of the world.

The origin of this 'simple and elegant' Theory, as Professor Hawking calls it, lies in a deep and contemplative mind – a mind which wondered why the stars twinkle or how it would be to travel with the speed of light. In Einstein's own words he discovered this theory because he was firmly convinced of the harmony of the Universe.

In 1905, when Albert Einstein was 26 years old, he published five research papers in the Scientific Journal *Annalen der Physik (Vol. 17).* Three of these papers are of special importance.

Einstein's curiosity to know about light and its nature is the subject matter of one: in this paper, which is commonly known as the 'Photo-electric Paper', Einstein developed Maxwell's Photo-electric Law, which dealt with the conversion of light energy into electric energy, and vice versa. This is the basis of telecommunications technology. It was a new way of looking at electro-magnetic radiation which was to become characteristic of the Quantum Theory, worked out and completed some twenty years later by a team of Physicists. For his contribution Einstein was awarded the Nobel Prize in 1921.

In the second paper, entitled 'Is the Inertia of a Body Dependent upon Its Energy Content?', Einstein proved that matter and energy were not two separate things, and that Matter could be converted into Energy, and Energy into Matter.

By far the most important of Einstein's papers was one entitled 'Electro-Dynamics of Moving Bodies' – a very unattractive title, but which brought about a veritable revolution in the world of physics. It explains in thirty pages what is now know as the Special Theory of Relativity. It is the deduction and formulation of laws from observation of facts when objects move through Space and Time.

In 1915 Albert Einstein developed the General Theory of Relativity. Einstein's reputation as a scientist is unique as, besides his other great contributions, he was the sole and only discoverer of this theory. Briefly and very simply, in this theory the framework of the Special Theory, which is principally based on the nature of light, is extended to include Gravity. It is now commonly known as the Theory of Gravity. Einstein developed this theory by considering the beam of light as a universal measuring standard.

Einstein got the inspiration of the General Theory from the realization that a person inside a falling lift whose cable had snapped would not feel gravity at all. And this could only be possible if gravity and acceleration are exactly equivalent to each other – that is, the acceleration of the falling lift speeding up with every second exactly cancels out the influence of gravity.

Newton's Law of Gravity does not explain what Gravity *is*. In *Philosophiæ Naturalis Principia Mathematica,* Newton actually states that a true understanding of the nature of gravity was beyond comprehension. Einstein's General Theory of Relativity explains the force of gravity in terms of the curvature of 4-dimensional Space-Time. According to him Gravity is not a force like other forces, but is consequence of the fact that Space-Time is not flat, as had been previously assumed, but is 'curved' or 'warped' by the distribution of mass and energy in it.[1]

In General Theory, Space and Time are considered as dynamic qualities. As Hawking put it, when a body moves or a force acts, it affects the curvature of space and time, and in turn the structure of space-time affects the way in which the bodies move and forces act. Space and time not only affect, but also are affected by, everything that happens in the Universe. In simple words, whenever there is a massive body there will also be a gravitational field, and this field will manifest itself as the curvature of space surrounding that body. In Einstein's theory, then, matter cannot be separated from its field of gravity, and the field of gravity cannot be separated from the curved space. Matter and space are thus seen to be inseparable and inter-dependent parts of a single whole.[2]

Einstein's General Theory predicted, as was proved in 1919, that a beam of light from distant stars passing close to the sun, would bend as it moved through Space-Time distorted by the sun's mass. Thus in Relativity Physics, Euclidian straight lines have to be replaced by light-rays. We cannot, in fact, find a place where Euclidian geometry is exactly true.

Einstein arrived at the exact equations governing the theory of Gravity, in which Space, Time and Matter were unified. It goes far beyond Newton's theory as it covers the whole Universe by including Space-Time. According to Einstein's equation, the material Universe could not be static, as Newton believed. This fact was confirmed by Edwin Hubble, the American astronomer, who in 1929 made the landmark observation, using a new and powerful telescope on a mountain-top in California, that the Universe is expanding.

This indicated that some 15 or 20 billion years ago the galaxies, constituting millions of stars, were on top of one another. In 1970 a joint paper by Professor Hawking and Roger Penrose proved that at this point of time there must have been a Big Bang singularity. This deduction was subject to the two important provisos that (a) the Theory of Relativity is correct (this is debatable), and (b) the Universe contains as much matter as we observe.

In November 1915, Einsten first communicated the basic equations of his theory to the Berlin Academy. He wrote that 'scarcely anyone who has fully understood this theory can escape from its magic.' In the historic meeting of 6 November 1919, of the London Royal Society and Royal Astronomical Society, J. J. Thomson, President of the Royal Society, described Einstein's General Theory of Relativity as 'one of the greatest – perhaps *the* greatest – of achievements in the history of human thought.' In 1968 P. A. M. Dirac described the General Theory of Relativity as 'probably the most beautiful of all existing physical theories'.

With these very brief and elementary remarks on the General Theory, let us make an attempt to consider the framework of the Special Theory of Relativity (propounded in 1905) on which the Theory of Gravity is based.

It should be pointed out to begin with, that the Theory of Relativity does not repudiate laws of nature that were discovered by earlier physicists. It is only their range of application which is now more clearly defined. The Special Theory of Relativity does not replace Newtonian Mechanics, which are still valid in the case of stationary objects or objects which move at the same speed in a straight line. For example, in a train travelling at a constant speed along a straight line, the motion of bodies inside the carriage is the same as in a stationary train – that is, everything inside a moving train, jolts apart, behaves exactly as if the train were at rest.

This is the important principle of relative motion. It says that the motion of bodies within frames that move uniformly and rectilinearly, relative to each other is governed by the same laws. The principle of the relativity of motion states that a body which is not acted upon by an external force may be either in a state of rest or in a state of rectilinear and uniform motion – a condition which physicists call the Law of Inertia. We owe the discovery of this law to Galileo, who showed that it was friction which brought moving bodies to a standstill, and that without friction, a body, once put into motion, would keep moving for ever. Newton's equation of motion is based on this principle.

In essence, the Special Theory is the result of a marriage between Newton's equation of motion and Maxwell's equation of electromagnetism, which describes the behaviour of radiation and light. The constancy of the speed of light, as we shall see later, plays an important and basic role in the Special Theory of Relativity.

The Theory is not as complicated as it sounds or is generally made out to be. It comprises a set of simple facts on observations made by Einstein of Phenomena, in case of rapid relative motion involving velocities approaching the speed of light.

It was not Einstein's idea to call this theory a Theory of Relativity. He did not like this name as according to him it sounded too complicated for a set of facts that are really quite simple. To my mind it is misnomer to call the Theory a Theory of Relativity. It is not a theory that everything is relative. This is a meaningless concept unless it is related to something which is constant and absolute. We cannot relate anything to earth as earth does not move along in a straight line, but is rotating round the sun at a speed of 30km per second and the sun itself is moving towards a point in the constellation Hercules. Similarly as we shall see that time and space are also not absolute and constant, but are a relative concept.

What then is constant and absolute to which things and events can be related so as to give them a mathematically correct meaning?

Thus, in essence the Special Theory of Relativity is not about what is relative. It is, to my mind, Einstein's search and discovery of something which is constant and absolute in the midst of our relative existence.

And Einstein discovered Light to be that absolute.

Chapter Eleven

THE THEORY OF RELATIVITY – II

Light

THE SPECIAL THEORY of Relativity is primarily based on the nature of light which plays a basic and fundamental role. It has been demonstrated that at the speed of light the laws of mechanics are no longer valid. They must be replaced by the laws of relative theory.

What is light and what is its nature? Is light a wave phenomenon or a particle phenomenon? According to Newton, light consists of small particles; Christian Huygens, a Dutch contemporary of Newton, proposed that light is, like sound, a wave phenomenon. The wave theory of light triumphed when it became clear that light is simply a particular form of electromagnetic wave. We owe this conclusion to James Clerk Maxwell's (1831–79) equations of the Electromagnetic field. The unique speed which Maxwell's equations established turned out to be exactly the speed of light which revealed that light must be a form of electromagnetic wave like radio waves but with shorter wave length. That was the position in the nineteenth century.

According to Einstein, mass is merely congealed energy, energy only liberated mass. From his observations of the behaviour of photons[1] – particles which had shed their mass and were travelling at the speed of light in the form of energy – Einstein in 1905 concluded that the propagation of light is both a wave process and a particle process.

This wave-particle duality changed our whole view of the nature of light. It contributed to the development of Quantum Theory, which constitutes the behaviour of atoms, particles and light.

Besides its particle-wave nature, there are other elements of light which play an important role in life and nature.

1) The speed of light (300,000km per second) is a universal constant of nature. It remains constant regardless of its source. It also remains constant regardless of the motion of the observer – that is, if the idea of universal time is abandoned, all observers should measure the same speed of light, no matter how fast they are moving.

2) The speed of light is absolute. From experiments in 1881, Albert Abraham Michelson (1852–1931)[2] discovered that on the rotating earth, light travelled in all directions at the same constant velocity. In other words, light's velocity of 300,000km per second is identical in every reference system. It is a universal constant of nature, absolute and not relative.

3) Light can neither be accelerated nor decelerated. Whatever changes or distortions the beam of light undergoes in matter, it propagates with the same velocity as soon as it emerges into a vacuum. If, for example, a plate of glass is placed in the path of a beam of light, the beam, after passing through the glass at a slower speed, on emergence regains the speed of 300,000km per second.

4) Light does not propagate instantaneously. It takes a beam of light eight minutes to travel the ninety-three millions miles from the sun to the earth. Similarly a beam of light takes one minute to travel from the moon to the earth. And it can take many light years[3] to reach the earth from distant stars. If the velocity of light had been infinite and instantaneous, Newton's Theory of Gravity could be considered to be as exact as the exact equations governing the General Theory of Relativity in which Einstein unified Space, Time and Matter. This is simply because if light were to be infinite and instantaneous, the concept of simultaneousness become absolute, and also the time intervals between events and body dimensions regardless of the frame from which they are observed.[4]

5) Speed of light has its limits and acts as a limiting velocity for all material objects. According to Einstein speed of light is a universal and fundamental constant of nature and the existence of the limiting velocity lies in the very nature of things. It is not possible for a material object to move through space at a speed equal to or greater than the speed of light; nor it is possible to accelerate a material object to the speed of light as it would take infinite energy to do so. It is because as an object approaches the speed of light, its mass increases, so it takes more and more energy to speed it further. It can never reach the speed of light, because by then its mass would have become infinite. Thus, all objects move at a lesser speed than light. Only light or other waves that have no intrinsic mass, can move at the speed of light but can never exceed it.

Radio waves propagate at the velocity of light. We have beaten the speed of sound by our supersonic aircraft, but it would not be possible to have 'superlight' telegraphy to send signals at velocities greater than the velocity of light, or even simultaneously, because of the limiting speed and the nature of time which is not absolute.

Thus the speed of light is not only the speed of a phenomenon which is an immutable law of Nature, but it plays an important part by virtue of it being a limiting velocity. Light either outstrips all other phenomena or arrives simultaneously with them.

It is because of the limiting speed of light that astronomers are able to discover and detect new stars and planets 'swimming into the ken' many millions of light-years away, some of which may possibly have collapsed and become extinct by now. Similarly it can be safely assumed that astronomers will discover in the near or distant future new stars, very many more light-years away than the stars already discovered, whose light may still be on its way to reach the earth.

Space and Time

The Theory of Relativity has revolutionized the concept of space and time. It puts an end to Newton's conception of absolute space and absolute time.

For Newton, the idea of absolute space had a mystic meaning. He considered it as eternal, infinite, immobile and all-present, that it can never be created or destroyed. 'It is absolute, in its own nature, without relation to anything external'; that is, it was homogeneous, isotropic and independent of matter. Similarly, as stated in the

Principia, time, like space, is universal, it has a homogeneous structure and, like space, is independent of matter. 'Absolute, true, and mathematical time,' as Newton put it, 'of itself and from its own nature, flows equally, without relation to anything external, and by another name is called duration.'[5]

Einstein's Theory of Relativity mathematically formulates the union of space and time which cannot be considered as separate.

All things move in space and time. But what exactly is space and what causes the flow of time? Is time a function of space or space a function of time?

What is time? Inexorably and relentlessly it ticks away. In a twinkle present becomes past and future becomes present. Time moves on. It moves on in space. It is related to motion which, in turn, is related to mass, energy and inertia. Thus time, space, mass and energy are inextricably mixed up. Space is not separate from time. Both constitute what Einstein calls the Space-Time continuum. As demonstrated by Einstein, space-time is not flat but is curved by the matter and energy in it.

Space and time are no longer considered as the passive background against which events take place, but as participants in the functioning of the scheme of things in the Universe. They are dynamic qualities that not only influence events but are influenced by them.

Another peculiarity of time, according to Einstein, is that, unlike light which has a universal speed, there is no such thing as universal flow of time; that is to say time is not a universal quality which exists on its own, separate from space. Time depends on the state of motion of the observer and moves at different rates for different observers. Thus every man carries with him his own space and his own time – called space-time.

In the words of the British astronomer, Sir Arthur Stanley Eddington (1882–1944), 'distance and duration are the most fundamental terms in physics – velocity, acceleration, force, energy, and so on, all depend on them; and we can scarcely make any statement in physics without direct and indirect reference to them.'

Distance is measured between two points, time by an experience. According to this Theory although distance and time vary for different observers, we can derive from them the quantity called 'interval' which is the same for all observers. To reproduce the words of Bertrand Russell: 'the world which the Theory of Relativity presents to our imagination is not so much a world of "things" in "motion" as a world of *events*... It is *events* that are the stuff of relativity physics.'[6]

There being no basic difference between space and time, a change in the state of motion of the observer implies a change in the structure of space. Einstein has demonstrated that in the case of objects moving at rapid speed, time dilation and space contraction are facts which form part of the mechanism of the Universe we live in. They are direct consequences of the universality of the speed of light. The speed of light, as a fundamental constant of nature, is rooted in the very structure of space-time.

For example, to a fast-moving observer a 30cm-long ruler would appear much shorter than its actual length.

This would not be an optical illusion, as all measuring instruments will be similarly effected. It must, however, be pointed out that space contraction applies only in the direction in which the observer is moving. The contraction of space manifests itself at the atomic level as well. It has been demonstrated that atoms appear to be flattened in the direction in which they move.

As regards time dilation it can be observed that a clock in motion, say in an airliner, would run more slowly than a stationary clock. It would come to a virtual standstill if the airliner were to approach the speed of light. In other words time itself will slow down for one in motion and come to a standstill on his reaching the speed of light.

Thus it is the peculiarity of Light that physically and metaphysically it can lead one to the state of timelessness!

Space has three dimensions. It gives us three different directions of motion: up and down, back and forth, right and left. It has, therefore, three coordinates. We can move in space at will from one place to another. Time, on the other hand, is considered as one-dimensional. It runs only in one direction – into the future. It has, therefore, only one coordinate. Unlike in space, we cannot move at will in time, because it ticks away beyond our control.

Thus, space-time constitutes four dimensions and has four coordinates. In the words of Hawking, why space-time should be four-dimensional is a question that is normally considered to be outside the realm of physics.

We can understand the Universe only by the coordinates of space and time. Without these coordinates an event is non-existent. In fact, without these coordinates corporeal existence is not possible. Time means duration. Space is the background in which events take place. Thus, events in space without time are non-existent. Without the duration of even a split second there cannot be any experience of pain or pleasure, joy or sorrow, as one is then in a state of timelessness.

Mass and Energy

The most important consequence of the union between space and time is the interchangeability of mass and energy. They are now closely related.

In classical or rather in Newton's physics, mass and energy are two separate concepts – the basis of the mechanics of Newton's physics being the stability and immutability of mass.

According to Einstein's hypothesis there is no fundamental difference between mass and energy – all mass being merely congealed energy and all energy merely liberated matter. Even an object at rest has energy stored in its mass. As an example the energy of a stationary car is zero. But when driven at the speed of say 100km per hour its kinetic energy as calculated by the equation $E=\frac{1}{2}mv^2$ becomes tremendous. The damage done by an impact at this speed would be somewhat similar to a fall of a person from the second floor of a building. If motorists were to be fully conscious of the consequences of accidents at such speeds, we would have much fewer accidents than at present.

Einstein postulates that mass can be converted into

energy and energy into mass. That transformation is described by his famous equation $E=mc^2$ (c being the speed of light).

The velocity of light being 300,000km per second, a small amount of mass, according to the equation, is equivalent to an enormous corresponding quantity of energy. This explains the continuing production of light and heat by our sun for billions of years while losing only a small amount of mass. Using Einstein's equation it is calculated that the mass lost by the sun per second is only four million tons.[7]

The sun, which has been in existence for more than four billion years, is our greatest nuclear reactor. It is burning by fusing hydrogen into helium like a controlled H-bomb. The temperature in the sun is so high that the present amount of matter converted into energy will so continue with its chain reaction for another five billion years or so before it runs out of nuclear fuel.

This interchangeability of small mass into enormous energy is the basis of nuclear power, commonly known as atomic phenomena. It is the secret underlying the atom bomb, which was first detonated by the USA in a New Mexico desert on 16 July 1945 – a date which will be remembered in the annals of history as the beginning of the nuclear age.

The first bomb was dropped, by the order of President Harry Truman, on 6 August 1945 on the Japanese harbour city of Hiroshima; the second, three days later, on Nagasaki, causing massive destruction. The two bombs killed more than 220,000 people. In the first, only about one gram of its mass was suddenly changed into energy by fission – producing an explosion equivalent to approximately 12,400 tons of the conventional explosive TNT.[8] This was a relatively ordinary and small uranium bomb as compared to the number of more powerful bombs at present in the arsenals of world powers, which are enough to destroy the world ten times over.

The nuclear phenomenon is not only at work in the sun, but in all the twinkling stars we see in the sky. The stars twinkle because they, like the sun, generate their own light by converting mass into radiation. The light from our sun, which is a second- or third-generation star, does not twinkle because it is so close to us. Nor does the light from the planets, which is steady, because the planets do not generate their own light but reflect it from the sun.

The relation between mass and energy is by far the most important aspect of the Theory of Relativity. We have seen that light transfers mass which, according to Einstein, is nothing but frozen energy. Similarly the mass of a body increases with its speed and when the body is nearing the speed of light (c) it tends to become infinite. Calculations also show that the mass of a moving body increases as much as its length diminishes. For example, if a football travelled at a very great speed, it would increase in mass and get flattened.

The equation $E=mc^2$ is the greatest contribution Einstein has made to the world of science. It is both a blessing and a curse. It holds the key to the transcendental transformation or to the annihilation of the whole world. It gives a clue to the power and potential of man, the crown of creation, who could harness unlimited energy from the sun as also from the stars with which the Cosmos eternally throbs.

The equation $E=mc^2$ not only gives a clue to the production of energy which can be generated from a small amount of mass but its corollary gives an equation for mass that is $m=E/c^2$; and that a beam of light is pure energy ($c=E/mc$).

Mass is one of the most important properties of a body. There is a subtle difference between mass and matter. Strictly speaking, as commonly understood, mass is not the quantity of matter a body contains. It is also not, as commonly understood, strictly constant. It is mixed up with energy. Being mutually convertible it is possible to create mass out of energy which is nothing but congealed energy as energy in fact is measured mass.

Newton gave a hint of this very idea when in his *Optics* he stated that 'the changing Bodies into Light, and Light into Bodies, is very comfortable to the very Course of Nature, which seems delighted with Transmutations'. This explains the phenomena, not uncommon in the Indian Yogic world, of levitation or dematerializing a body and materializing it at some other place.

In this context it may be appropriate to reproduce the following passage by Michael Collins which forms part of his Foreword to *Our Universe*:

> Beyond Pluto, we have to admit that the distances seem to be too much for us, at least if we regard the velocity of light as the universal speed limit. However, not too many years ago, experts believed we would

> never break the sound 'barrier'. Right now, Einstein's theories seem to deny us the stars. Perhaps some day we can discover how to disembody humans in one place and recreate them elsewhere, to circumvent Einstein's barrier, and to roam the Universe seeking our peers or our superiors.

We are all bits of the sun and have similar self-renewing energy which can be discovered and successfully practised by yogic disciplines, thereby making it possible for man to live a normal, active and useful life for 150 years. Some take the view that brain cells start to die without renewal with the onset of age, and completely die out at the age of 125 years. Individual experience would tell us that this is not so. Brain cells get renewed and developed by remaining in contact with the Eternal, which is the source of all energy. And man alone is capable of becoming and remaining conscious of That – the All-Pervading and Self-evolving Consciousness.

The Timeless in man has made him timeless and it is given to man to bring this awareness of timelessness in his life and be aglow with freshness and vitality ever waking up with the freshness of Eternal dawn. Besides other disciplines, faith, value-based motivation and Anchor are necessary to help one fulfil his life and deny old age.

The power that created the Universe is latent in all its creation.

> A grain of sand, a simple atom
> Is mighty as the whirling winds
> As mighty as the heaving oceans,
> And mighty as the Mind of Man.

In other words, a human body properly trained and disciplined is capable of developing into an atomic reactor and performing miracles which, in reality, are nothing but the Cosmic Laws yet to be unfolded.

However, the less sceptical and more realiztic and practical approach would be to apply our minds to the constructive possibilities not beyond the scope of Physics. It is, for example, not beyond the ingenuity of Science to construct a Nuclear Reactor on earth a veritable Power-house of the World – based on the principle of fusion which, by its controlled chain reaction of thermonuclear combustion, could continue to convert our unlimited supply of hydrogen or more practically deuterium into helium, of which there is a plentiful supply on earth. To quote Harald Fritzsch, 'There is a plentiful supply of fusion fuel, especially deuterium, on Earth. All the energy needed by a country as large as the United States for one day could easily be generated by the fusion of a mere 250 kilograms of deuterium and tritium'.[9]

We could thus produce for countless years much more than our needs of power and energy, light and heat and what else for the entire human race. This would be a more constructive approach than directing our energies to producing more powerful and destructive weapons like the Hydrogen bomb.

Chapter Twelve

THE THEORY OF RELATIVITY – III

> Science has a long way to develop yet; of *that* I am certain!
>
> Roger Penrose – *Shadows of the Mind*

The Scope of Science – New Dimensions

I AM NOT A PHYSICIST. Possessing a rudimentary knowledge of science, much less of Mathematics I have in the foregoing pages given my understanding, as gleaned from knowledge sources, of the Theory of Relativity. I have avoided mathematical formulations and the intricacies of equations involved in the General Theory. I find it more fascinating to look at the trail-blazing cloud against the background of the beautiful blue than to be in that cloud.

The measure of scientific progress and achievements since the times of Galileo Galilei is that today the world is viewed by physicists in terms of two incompatible, partial and incomplete theories: Relativity and Quantum Mechanics. This is the summit of the achievement of twentieth-century Physics.

So far, science has not been able to go beyond the paradigm of particle and wave, or to cross the barrier of the Uncertainty Principle of Quantum Mechanics, much less to reconcile and combine the two theories into a single consistent Theory of Quantum Gravity. Physicists are still striving to formulate the Grand

Unified Theory (GUT) or Theory of Everything (ToE), which was the dream of Einstein and remains so of other scientists.

Our objective is to go beyond the present frontier of Physics and find an answer to the ever enigmatic question of the why and wherefore of the world and of the reality behind the Universe. Man is not only interested in the Universe but is interested in life, its inevitability, its meaning, and its relation to the Universe. This in fact is the eventual aim of all progressive institutions of Art and Literature, Science and Religion, Physics and Philosophy. There is no East and West in sorrow or fear. The problem and the aim are universal – suffering, the end of suffering, and the sublimation of human life.

According to Hawking, Quantum Mechanics and Relativity are known to be inconsistent with each other – they cannot both be correct.

The Theory of Relativity is a classical theory based on light as the measuring standard which, according to Einstein, is a universal constant of nature. In 1970 a joint paper by Hawking and Roger Penrose proved that *if* the Theory of Relativity is correct then there should be space-time singularities. And, as reckoned by the cosmologists, there was in fact a Big Bang singularity some 15 billion years ago when the Universe along with space and time had its beginning. The Theory of Relativity regards the world as a continuum. It does not take into account Quantum Theory which introduces an element of unpredictability and randomness.

The Quantum Theory was completed a few years

after the Theory of Relativity. According to Hawking, it is undoubtedly the greatest achievement of theoretical physics in this century, basic postulate of which is the Heisenberg Uncertainty Principle. Quantum Mechanics is a theory of perception. It does not describe the world in terms of particle and wave. It also does not predict a singularity like the Big Bang. On closer study of Quantum Mechanics, the great American physicist Richard Feynman, well known for his work on the Quantum Theory of Light, developed a more pragmatic approach to the subject as a result of which we have the concept of 'sum-over histories' or 'path integral'. The 'sum-over histories' means that a system does not have just a single history in space-time and that particles can take *any* path through space-time and possibly travel faster than light.[1] Thus the Universe could have all possible histories.

Professor Hawking, applying Feynman's 'sum-over-historics' approach to Big Bang singularity, proposed in the late 1970s that the Universe is completely self-contained. It is without beginning and without end. It is neither created nor destroyed. It just is. If so, asks Hawking, 'what place then for a Creator?'[2]

This concept of a Universe without beginning and without end, as argued in the earlier chapter 'On Consciousness', comes near to Oriental thinking. Differing from Hawking's idea of a personal Creator, the Oriental concept of Brahma curiously echoes the words of the Bible, that the All-Pervading Spirit, without beginning and without end, brooding over its own Omnipresence and Omniscience, 'the same yesterday, and today, and for ever,'[3] existed, exists and will continue to exist 'even unto the end of the world'.[4]

By 1927, the foundations of the new Physics, Quantum Mechanics and Relativity were in place. The scientists having been unsuccessful for nearly 70 years to reconcile and combine the two irreconcilable and incomplete theories, it may perhaps be worthwhile to consider a proposition which may possibly help achieve the aim of enlightened Physics. One cannot but be very reluctant to intrude where more knowledgeable men would fear to tread. We are confronting the ineffable. And according to Max Planck, father of Quantum Mechanics, poetic intuition is more likely to comprehend the aim of science which intellect can never fully grasp.[5] The mind and intellect cannot comprehend that which is above and beyond mind and intellect. Direct experience is the only valid confirmation which can be perceived and experienced at the higher level of Consciousness.

At that basic and higher level Universe is a harmonious whole, a glimpse of which one can have at times. There is a uniformity in diversity. There is balance and power, elegance and rhythm.

At this plane it should not be difficult to reconcile the two seemingly irreconcilable theories of 20th century physics. If there is no road, an earnest traveller makes a road by walking on the way to the Goal.

To achieve our objective to combine the Theory of Relativity and Quantum Mechanics and produce a consistent Unified Field Theory, it is important, first and foremost, to examine whether the Theory of Relativity is correct.

The Theory of Relativity is principally based on the nature of light which plays a fundamental role as the universal measuring tool in Physics. According to Einstein the two important and basic assumptions regarding light are that:

(a) nothing in the Universe can travel faster than the speed of light, and

(b) it is a universal constant of nature.

It is proposed that the very premise on which the Theory of Relativity is based is wrong. Light is neither the fastest phenomenon in the world nor is it a universal constant of nature.

In an earlier chapter, while discussing Bell's Theorem and Bohm's Hypothesis, it was argued that faster-than-light communication, of a type different from conventional Physics, between two objects separated by space-like distance is a distinct possibility. In fact, the thought experiments of Einstein, Podolsky and Rosen (known as the EPR effect) demonstrated that information can be communicated at super-luminal (faster than light) speeds. This has now become an integral aspect of our physical reality. Telepathy is an example in point which often appears to happen instantaneously. It shows that there is a continuity of mind – the individual minds being fragments of the Universal Mind like waves in the ocean. As there is no break in the waters of the river, there is no break in matter. On account of this continuity we can instantaneously convey our thoughts directly to another, even though separated by thousands of miles.

Another, perhaps more obvious, example is that of thought which can beat the speed of light. This aspect of thought has already been discussed in an earlier chapter. In a split second, thought can reach any town or country anywhere in the world. It can reach the sun and the moon and survey the entire Universe with galaxies of stars millions of light years away.

What is thought? Is it a wave or a particle? It could perhaps give the result of both in varying circumstances.

Thought, like a beam of light, is pure energy. It is a pulsating force somewhat akin to photons, the light quanta, which have shed their mass but are always travelling with the speed of light. Thought is faster. Unlike light, thought can make a probe into a black hole without being trapped by its field of gravity. Light transfers mass but thought centred in Consciousness can bring about a veritable change in the entire Universe. As earlier stated, mind-thought, space-time and Consciousness are interwoven – an interrelationship which makes possible the existence of the phenomenal world as we see it. Let thought cease, and there is neither time nor space.

So far, no equation similar to $E=mc^2$, which involves the speed of light, has been formulated involving the speed of thought – an equation which may possibly result in something more unique than harnessing of atomic energy. It may give us a glimpse of Reality, its power and its potential and develop man into a superman with the freedom of the entire Universe. Thought can lead one to merge into pure Consciousness – the Ultimate Reality where the world of duality, of pleasure and pain, good and evil, death and life, cause and effect disappear and man becomes his own destiny.

As regards the second assumption regarding light, it

is proposed that neither thought nor light are constants of nature. A beam of light undergoes a change when passing through matter. If, for example, a plate of glass is placed in the path of a beam of light it will slow down. The same is true of thought: depending on various factors it can go slow or fast.

Light is fast. But faster than light is thought. And faster even than thought is the All-Pervading Consciousness. Consciousness, by virtue of its being All-Pervading, is the fastest phenomenon in the Universe. And it is the one and only constant of nature. It is not time-bound. Whatever is time-bound has a beginning and an end. But Consciousness is the same 'today, yesterday, and for ever'.

Body, mind, and intellect are rooted in consciousness. Consciousness is the essence – a living principle in which the whole world moves and has its being. It is the key to the mystery of life and death. It is the key to our very existence. In fact, the entire Universe is a cosmos of Consciousness – the Ocean in which all waves exist and dissolve.

This is not to negate the world. It is to see the world as appearing in Consciousness as the totality of the known in the immensity of the Unknown.

This is how modern Physics has begun to view the phenomenal world. According to Quantum Mechanics, there is no such thing as objectivity. It has been argued by Eugene Winger that it was not possible to formulate the laws of Quantum Theory in a fully consistent way without reference to consciousness, and that the explicit inclusion of human consciousness may be an essential aspect of future theories of matter.[6] For quite some time modern Physics has tended to become the study of the structure of Consciousness.

Einstein has demonstrated that matter is the same thing as energy. And going by Bell's Theorem and David Bohm's hypothesis, discussed in an earlier chapter, space-time, mass-energy, mind-thought, cause-effect form part of the Totality in which the past, present and future histories of the Universe are contained, like waves in an ocean of Consciousness.

What is Relativity?

The same lamp that is bright by night is dim by day. In 1955, when Einstein was asked to explain Relativity, he replied, 'when you sit with a nice girl for two hours, you think it's only a minute. But when you sit on a hot stove for a minute, you think it's two hours. That's relativity.'[7]

It follows from the foregoing that Relativity involves both time and thought, which in turn depend on the state of one's mind. And mind can stop or advance the flow of time. In other words, as in Quantum Mechanics, subjectivity plays an important role in Relativity. Thus Consciousness, in which thought and mind are rooted, plays the fundamental role in both theories and it is at this level that their inconsistency can be resolved and reconciled.

We live and have our being in three conditioned states – body (the state of perceptions and actions), mind (emotions and feelings) and intellect (thoughts and ideas). Most of our lives are spent in waking, dreaming and deep sleep states. But beyond these three states there is a fourth state, known as Turya in Sanscrit. It is the state of Pure Consciousness which projects the Universe of matter and energy, space and time, particles and waves, of thoughts, feelings, emotions and imagination. In other words, our world is a world of Relativity and Quantum Mechanics which is rooted in the Self, the Absolute, the All-Pervading Consciousness which like the beam of Light through the prism of *Prakriti* (nature) has projected the phenomenal world of many-coloured hues and of various names and forms. It can thus be stated that not only this world but the entire Universe can be contained in the framework of Quantum Mechanics and the General Theory of Relativity (which takes due account of gravity), with Consciousness as the Universal Constant. Without taking Consciousness into account, the Unified Field Theory, the Theory of Everything (ToE) or Grand Unified Theory (GUT) cannot possibly be formulated.

We have been going round and round the obvious, unable to discover the Reality which all along has been right with us.

> The centre that I cannot find
> Is known to my Unconscious Mind
> I have no reason to despair
> Because I am Already There.[8]

By reconciling and combining the two theories it does not necessarily follow that there was no Big Bang singularity. Such singularities are not infrequent. In fact, every Black Hole is an example of such singularity. In the words of Hawking, the Big Bang resembles a black-hole explosion but on a vastly larger scale.[9]

Such singularities are taking place in the Cosmos and Universes beyond Universes are being created and dissolved. Consider the Andromeda galaxy, which is closest to our own, about 2.5 million light years from Earth. There is every reason to believe thousands of solar systems exist much like our own.[10] And on the formation of different solar systems, with varying fields of gravity, time with different beginning and different divisions of hours and minutes, will have altogether a different connotation than ours.

Consciousness reigns supreme. This Omnipotent, All-Pervading, High Intelligence, without beginning and without end, will continue to exist for ever. Thus, every Big Bang singularity may be conceived and compared to a wave in the boundless and fathomless Ocean of that Consciousness. In that sense, the Universe and consequently time is without beginning and will have no end – the present moment of timelessness being the measure of Eternity.

It has been earlier stated that the Theory of Relativity, which takes light as the universal constant, has altered the hitherto-held views by the physicists of the fundamental structure of the world. The nature of light, *inter alia*, being that:

1) it transfers mass, which can become infinite

2) it dilates time, and can lead one to the state of timelessness

3) it can be the source of unlimited energy as formulated by the equation $E=mc^2$.

Try and conceive the structure of the world with the poet's eye, by replacing Consciousness – the Absolute –

for light as the universal constant in our relative existence. The entire complexion of the world changes. It is transformed into many-coloured splendour. We enter the radiant realm of light and power, beauty and sublimity, which language cannot describe. Time-space, mass-energy, acquire a new meaning. We *see* things as mystics do. The ordinary world of name and form disappears. It is no longer fragmented. We *see* it as a seamless whole. There is One and the only One that manifests itself in countless shapes and forms. Space-time dissolves into the vast and unfathomable Ocean of Bliss and we are transported into a state of timeless present which transcends the realms of mind and intellect.

It is time that scientists were to capture and formulate such experiences of Beauty and Sublimity by *perceiving* the Reality which, according to the Copenhagen Interpretation, lies beyond the capabilities of rational thought.

Einstein had the right perception when he said: 'Nature hides her secret because of her essential loftiness, but not by means of ruse.'[11] The modern scientist has to raise himself to that level of loftiness to be able to comprehend what at present seems incomprehensible.

Einstein's lifelong aim was to search for the Truth, beneath the variations of relative appearances – a search for unity in diversity. To that end he kept all the doors of knowledge, both of physics and metaphysics, open to allow the free flow of thoughts and ideas.

When asked whether there was any relation between science and Metaphysics, Einstein declared that science itself was Metaphysics.[12] In his article on 'Religion and Science' which appeared on Sunday 9 November 1931 in the *New York Times Magazine*, he asserted that 'the cosmic religious experience is the strongest and noblest driving force behind scientific research.' And, as a corollary, 'the only deeply religious people of our largely materialistic age are the earnest men of research.'[13] According to him,

> science can only be created by those who are thoroughly imbued with the aspiration toward truth and understanding. This source of feeling, however, springs from the sphere of religion. To this there also belongs the faith in the possibility that the regulations valid for the world of existence are rational, that is, comprehensible to reason. I cannot conceive of a genuine scientist without that profound faith. The situation may be expressed by an image: Science without religion is lame, religion without science is blind.[14]

One cannot help but agree with Gary Zukav, when he observed that the language of eastern mystics and that of western physicists is becoming very similar.[15]

While discoursing on the dimensions of Mathematics, Roger Penrose, in his book *Shadows of the Mind,* refers to the Three Worlds and the mysteries that relate them one to another. The Three Worlds being, mental, physical and Platonic worlds of mathematical forms, suggesting that 'the ideal concept of "the good" or "the beautiful" must also be attributed a reality just as a mathematical concept must.' Penrose finally rounds up by saying that 'no doubt there are not really three worlds but *one*, the true nature of which we do not even glimpse at present'. Penrose is in fact referring to the 'one world' of Consciousness, which in Vedic language is known as Turya. It is at that level of Consciousness that Newton, Einstein, Archimedes, Galileo, Darwin, Leonardo da Vinci, Rembrandt, Picasso, Bach, Mozart, Plato and other great minds were capable of having the direct perception of Truth and Beauty – a faculty which is given us in lesser degree.

The state of Consciousness is the measure of man. Like waves in an ocean, we all have our being in that Ocean of Consciousness which is ever vibrating with timeless energy. The more of ocean in the wave, the bigger the wave. This distinguishes men from men, persons from personalities.

A scientist's, a poet's or an artist's sincerity and intensity of feelings, his inspiration and depth of vision, as generated by the Supreme Consciousness, are the measures to judge the quality of his work.

This is the secret of great men and men of God – the heroes and the heroic in history, as Thomas Carlyle puts it. Such men live in the inward sphere of things, in the True, Divine and the Eternal – their whole being ever vibrating with the Cosmic Consciousness which gives them the power to sway the world. No one ever acquired enduring wealth and power, or achieved greatness or lasting fame, without that spiritual depth. All great men, knowingly or unknowingly, have it in them. To develop that depth, one has to go to the Great Reservoir by discovering which one gets everything in life. Seek it and you will find that Thou art That[16] – I AM THAT I AM.[17]

To go beyond the paradigm of particle and wave and to cross Heisenberg's barrier of uncertainty, science has to take a leap of faith to reach the Source which is the repository of absolute Truth and all knowledge.

One cannot but agree with Michael White and John Gribbin[18] that Stephen Hawking, one of the greatest minds of our time, aided, I think, by the great mathematician Roger Penrose, remains the most likely person to lead the way towards the formulation of a Grand Unified Theory (GUT), the Theory of Everything which has eluded scientists for the past 70 years.

However, for the present, we are left in doubt as to whether an equation is possible with the Absolute as its basic factor.

Chapter Thirteen

THE END OF PHYSICS AND PHILOSOPHY

THE TWO BASIC THEORIES of twentieth-century Physics – Quantum Mechanics and Relativity – have completely changed our world view, hitherto based on Cartesian thought and Newton's Physics. According to modern science the world is one whole, every particle of which is inter-connected. It reveals the basic oneness of the Universe and shows that mind, thought and consciousness are the essential parts of natural phenomena.

Ordinarily the world is seen by us a five-fold phenomenon of the five senses with the mind playing the role of perceiving it. Without the mind this world, which after all is a collection of memories, is non-existent. The scope, the power and the potential of the mind, which projects the world of thoughts and ideas, of dreams and of the seeming reality, has already been discussed in earlier chapters.

Our mind by nature is restless. It either dwells in the past or wanders into the future, but it seldom stays in the present. It is the nature of the mind to wander, but its Dharma[1] is to become still. Still the mind and there is peace. Ultimately it is the solitude of one's mind which gives meaning to human existence.

Besides the Physical world of Perceptions and actions,

mental and intellectual world of emotions and feelings, thoughts, ideas and imagination, there is the Transcendental world of Pure or Unconditioned Consciousness which constitutes the core. This is the Ultimate Reality which is the repository of all the basic and immutable laws which govern the Universe. And, as argued earlier, without Consciousness as the basic factor, Unified Field Theory cannot be formulated.

Combining Quantum Field Theory and Relativity means a formulation of a Theory of Totality. What is Totality? It is the Fundamental Force which underlies all the four basic forces as classified by physicists. It gives energy to the source of energy; it gives heat to the fire and makes it burn; it makes water flow, the wind blow and living beings breathe. It is the One and the only constant of Nature as pure or unconditioned Consciousness. It is the Reality which we are seeking behind the phenomenal world of change and relative existence.

It is difficult to grasp the concept of Reality, for it is beyond the comprehension of man's mind and intellect. It is better understood by its attributes and manifold manifestations. Try to imagine that the tip of a live incense stick can burn the whole world, or that a moment is Eternity and contains the whole of the past and creates the future, or that the One is the Many and the Many are the One. This gives some idea of the concept of Totality.

In an earlier chapter an attempt has been made to describe the nature of Reality. This concept has been developed more comprehensively in the Kaivalya Upanishad, which forms part of the Atharva Veda. It is a gem amongst the shorter Upanishads. It excels in poetic diction, systematic development of thought, and depth and subtlety of philosophy.

Reality is Supreme. It is Ineffable, Immutable, Eternal. It is Self-evolving and Self-effulgent. It is the All-Pervading, Omnipotent non-dual Brahma. It is subtler than the subtlest, greater than the greatest. It is the One and also the Many. It is beyond existence and non-existence. It is beyond Space, Time and Causation. It is Immaculate, without birth and death. It is without beginning and without end. It is supremely tranquil, perfectly blissful. It is the Immovable, which is the cause of all movement. It is the Formless which projects all forms – gross, subtle and supreme. It is High Intelligence. It is the Witness. It sees without eyes, hears without ears. It is the knowing principle by which all is known. It is the Manifold Universe. Like the rising and subsiding waves in an ocean, the Universe with various names and forms originates, exists and dissolves in that Reality.

Truth, Beauty, Bliss, and other such words are just pointers to give a glimpse of the power, potential, the radiance and immensity of That, commonly known as God. To contemplate Him is to enter the boundless region of the Profound. Man's mind is simply struck with wonder and awe at the blinding light of Transcendence.

It is doubtful whether an equation is at all possible with the Absolute as the basic factor which cannot be grasped or fully understood by man's mind and intellect.

The limitlessness of God is expressed in a form closer to the mathematical infinite by St Gregory. 'No matter how far our mind may have progressed in the contemplation of God, it does not attain to what He is, but to what is beneath Him.'[2]

In a lecture delivered on 29 April 1980,[3] when he was inaugurated as Lucasian Professor of Mathematics at Cambridge, Stephen Hawking envisaged the possibility of computers taking over theoretical Physics altogether, which may mean the end of theoretical Physicists. I can best express my views in the words of Rudy Rucker: 'Try to catch the Universe in a finite net of axioms and the Universe will fight back. Reality is, on the deepest level, essentially infinite. No finitely programmed machine can ever exhaust the richness of the mental and physical world we inhabit.'

Direct experience of Reality transcends the realms of thought and language. And it is the only valid confirmation which intellect, however rational, cannot comprehend.

Heaven and Hell are not geographical places but states of mind and experience. The goal of Vedanta, Sufism and Mysticism in general is to experience the All-Pervading Reality and to become one with it.

Although it is not possible to conceive, much less to describe, the Absolute, it is within man's reach to become it; just like a black ball of iron thrown into the furnace acquires the attributes of the fire or like a river which merges into the deep and unfathomable Ocean. The river loses its identity but gains the Totality. According to Kaivalya Upanishad, this unity can be achieved by faith, meditation and deep devotion, which are the same emotion as sublimated love.

By identifying oneself with the Eternal one acquires the attributes of the Eternal. There is no sliding back on reaching the sticking point. This means enlightenment. One becomes *Jeevan Mukta,* a Self-realized being who is liberated from all bonds, physical and mental. For him the night of dreams has ended. He has awakened to a new world of Light which casts no shadows. He is no longer bound by the world of name and form. He is beyond duality. He has outsoared the state of doubt and fear, love and hate, pleasure and pain, grief, sickness, old age and death.

During the span of his bodily existence, before he merges into the Infinitude of the Eternal, *Jeevan Mukta* has the freedom of the Universe. He can know and experience for himself all that exists. He can command, interfere with the workings of nature, change the chain of causation, and even undo the past. He has become his own destiny and is capable of changing the destinies of others. Neither time nor space exist for the one who knows the Eternal. For him there is no past or future. He lives in a state of timeless present. He desires nothing, for he is complete for ever. This is the perfect state. The evolution of man is complete. He has become the nature of the Eternal. He is illuminated. Here Physics and Philosophy, Science and Religion end.

When Plato could fully perceive the Good, his philosophy ended. Similarly it will be the end of Physics when scientists, at present baffled by Quantum uncertainty, are able to *perceive* the Source which is the repository of all the basic and immutable laws governing the Universe.

According to generally accepted anthropological findings, the anatomical evolution of human nature was virtually completed some fifty thousand years ago. Over the millennia how many Buddhas and Christs has the world produced? And how far has science progressed in discovering the basic and immutable laws of nature and the Reality behind the Universe?

Years and years have rolled by and with it ages unknown. Man's quest to know and understand life and Reality behind the Universe is never ending and I wonder if it will ever end. And this is what Godel's Theorem tells us: man will never know the final secret of the Universe.4

So sang Lord Tennyson: 'We know not anything. So many worlds, so much to do, so little done.'

> So runs my dream: but what am I?
>   An infant crying in the night:
>   An infant crying for the light:
> And with no language but a cry.[5]

And, thus wrote Henry Luce:

> We assert by faith one proposition: that life does have a meaning. We also acknowledge that the full meaning of human life touches the mysterious, even the mystical, because the Truth, the full Truth, about the human adventure for ever eludes our finite intelligence, however clever.[6]

Having heard the voices of poetry and theology, let us hear what Albert Einstein, one of the greatest scientists of our time, had to say in later years of his life: 'One thing I have learnt in a long life: that all our science, measured against reality, is primitive and child-like.'

It is also well to reproduce Dr Chaim Tschernowitz's vivid account of a summer trip with Einstein on the Havelsee during which their discussions were often metaphysical.

> The conversation (on Einstein's sailboat) drifted back and forth from profundities about the nature of God, the Universe and man, to lighter questions. Suddenly, Einstein lifted his head, looked up at the skies and said: 'We know nothing about it at all. Our knowledge is but the knowledge of school children.'
>
> 'Do you think', asked Dr Chaim Tschernowitz, 'that we shall ever probe the secret?'
>
> 'Possibly', he said with a movement of his shoulders, 'we shall know a little more than we do now. But the real nature of things, that we shall never know, never.'[7]

Amidst the noise and the bustle and the hum of life, there falls a hush when one suddenly becomes aware of the stillness of Silence. I see a procession of humanity marching along towards the inevitable end, the time of inevitability uncertain.

> At the edge of time and space, Eternity gapes
> A Void Great where Silence reigns supreme.

In the evening of my life, such as I am, I cannot do better than to conclude with what I wrote over a decade ago in my Journal:

> There is a Cosmic Life Force. It has intelligence. It has a purpose.
>
> The all-knowing, all-comprehending Intelligence

encompasses our thoughts and actions. It permeates the core of all sentient and non-sentient beings. It influences, shapes and fashions the affairs and destinies of men, nations and civilisations. It guides and governs the movements of sun, stars and planets. The Universe, as we know it or we do not know at present, conceivable and inconceivable cosmos, is the projection of the Life Force.

Life Force is ever working, perceptibly and imperceptibly, in accordance with the Mystic Law. It has its varied and manifold manifestations, comprehensible and incomprehensible at times. Joys and sorrows, happiness and misery, sin and its atonement, mercy, compassion, Divine Grace, Death and Immortality are within its dispensation.

The Essence of it all is sometimes perceived in one's consciousness, but cannot be fully expressed. Infinitude – beyond space and time. Eternity – a moment, a flash.

All of a sudden, my being is transported to regions unknown. Billions and billions of years seem to be compressed in a moment. I am aware, suddenly aware, of something of which unknowingly I have been its intrinsic part.[8]

Mystery is wrapped in mystery. A mysterious Power, benevolent and compassionate, surrounds us all. Complete self-surrender to that Will Supreme is liberation.

Away with Physics and Philosophy, Science and Scriptures,
Away with Newton's laws and Quantum's flaws
Away with Atoms and Photons, Quarks and Quasars
The unknown worlds and worlds and worlds afar.

Come my Beloved come
The moon is full, the stars are bright,
In the stillness of night, in the sacred Silence
Hear the heartbeats of the Cosmic rhythm.

Sweet mystery of life is wrapped in folds of love
Who is to question whom? Who is to answer whom?
The Universe of many-coloured hues
Radiant with Beauty is one harmonious whole
The One Eternal reigns supreme
With just a fragment of His splendour.

Chapter Fourteen

THE REALIZATION OF REALITY

> Each soul is potentially divine. The goal is to manifest this divine within, by controlling nature, external and internal. Do this either by work, or worship, or psychic control, or philosophy, by one, or more, or all of these – and be free. This is the whole of religion. Doctrines, or dogmas, or rituals, or books, or temple, or forms, are but secondary details.
>
> Swami Vivekananda

LIFE IS A PRECIOUS GIFT. It is the gateway to Freedom and Light. But it is seldom seen and experienced as a manifestation of colour and beauty, love and compassion.

We live in a sad world. It is impermanent, illusory – a place of pain, non-eternal. Here happiness is a mirage, which ever eludes us. And joy is only an interlude between continuing sufferings. And man and nature seem to have conspired to add to our woes.

There is hatred and violence. There have been two World Wars in one lifetime, bringing in their wake death, destruction, devastation and untold suffering. And wars persist.

There are personal tragedies, sorrow, pain and loss. There are accidents and epidemics, natural disasters and calamities – cyclonic storms, fires, floods and earthquakes.

What have we done to deserve all this? cries mankind

in its agony.

In his thought-provoking article, 'Why we need an Alternative Society', Arnold Toynbee wrote: 'Our increasing material affluence is leaving us unsatisfied, strained, restless and haunted by fear of being released by death from a life we do not enjoy.'[1]

There is fear and apprehension in man's mind, a sense of bewilderment at the state of our being and the inevitability of death which no one can escape.

What are we to do? How to escape this prison we call life and be free? Where is the way? In Eternal sleep, deep and dreamless? In death?

And how is one to face death? And after death what? To go through, according to Hindu and Buddhist concepts, the usual cycle of birth and death with all its inevitability of pain and sorrow, sickness and old age.

And how is one to face rebirth? What can one expect to be incarnated into? With his present make-up and the sum total of what he is, how can one hope to improve his position in his next incarnation, much less be an heir to the bliss and beatitude of life everlasting?

And common intelligence revolts against the logic of being born after death in an Arabian Night Heaven where rivers of wine flow and fairies abound and one could indulge in sensuous delights galore without a hangover, which follows dissipation and over-indulgence. A paradise like this, one could create anyhow, in this very life! But to what end? There is nothing permanent. Longest life of pleasure disappears like a flash.

Is man, then, like a hapless worm tossed about in

the turbulent ocean of existence, a mere creature of circumstances without a free will, born to live a life as ordained by nature on which he has no control?

Can we ever change our destiny? Can we ever conquer death and attain a state where there is no want, sorrow, suffering, sickness and old age – a state of permanent bliss and beatitude?

These are profound questions for which baffled humanity seeks an answer.

There must be a way out. In this world of duality, if there is a veil of ignorance which makes us fumble in the darkness and is the cause of our sufferings, there is also a door to knowledge which shows us the light of Truth and dispels darkness born of ignorance, leading us to a state of sublimity, of permanence and perfection.

Knock at the door and it shall be opened unto you.[2]

Most of us, ever busy in our day-to-day pursuits, seldom ask ourselves the questions:

Who am I? Where did I come from? Why do I exist? Where am I going to?

We are confused about the real and ultimate goal of life, which is Self-realization – to come face to face with Reality and be free.

On discovering the Truth, our life is fulfilled. We emerge from darkness to light, from bondage to liberation. Thereafter, there is no want, there is no sorrow, there is no death. No effort, no sacrifice, is therefore too great to reach that state of enlightenment.

The way to Realization of Reality is pathless. Truth is universal. No particular religion, creed, sect or system has a monopoly of it. There are as many ways to reach the sun as its rays. There are as many paths to reach Reality as there are human beings. Everyone has to seek and strive and search the Truth earnestly and diligently and, as exhorted by Lord Buddha, 'to be lamps unto themselves'.

Learn by investigation from one source or the other, from one religion or more, by service, by discipleship, by guidance and instructions from the wise and seers of essence of things.

It is the intensity and earnestness with which one seeks the Truth that matters.

> The gods approve
> The depth, and not the tumult, of the soul.[3]

Life is complex and varied. One's mind is bogged down with permutations and combinations of the ideas generated, possible ways suggested, precepts prescribed, codes of conduct and ethics laid down to seek and find the Truth.

Before one sets out on the path of Truth, the first and foremost requisite for the Realization of Reality is faith in the existence of Reality. Without faith in the Eternal, search is futile. 'All things are possible to him that believeth.'[4] 'The man consists of his faith: that which his faith is, he is even that.'[5]

Faith is blind. How is, for example, one to be convinced of the existence of any remote part, town or country, in the world which he has never seen without believing in the Atlas or in the account given or published by someone who has visited and seen the place? Similarly, one has to believe in the prophets, poets, saints and sages who have had direct experience and perception of Reality.

After Krishnamurti's discourse in Amsterdam in 1970, I asked, 'I can see Mount Everest, but how to reach it?'

'One who can see Mount Everest, will reach it one day', was his reassuring reply.

So, the first step towards our goal is to have firm faith in the Creator who became the Creation.

According to the Big Bang model of the Universe, all life on earth, all sentient beings and non-sentient things have a common origin. This establishes the link and kinship between man and his Creator, man and man, man and Nature. This very thought and conviction can dispel all darkness and doubt in man's mind and put an end to human suffering. The duality of 'I' and 'You' disappears. There can be no anger or fear, no hatred against anyone. Realization dawns that to hate and hurt others is to hate oneself. You feel whole – a part of the Universe and at one with Humanity. You realize in a flash that to love your neighbour is to love your own self, that the brotherhood of man is the corollary of the fatherhood of God. There is an end to sorrow.

Adams Beck[6] reproduces an episode in the life of Lord Buddha:

> One of his five original converts, Assaji, had gone into the town to ask for alms. A young Brahmin of noble birth named Sariputta saw him and having been moved by the dignity of his serene presence, asked him:
>
> 'Friend, your eyes shine. Your colour is pure and clear. Great is your composure. In whose name have you renounced the world and Who is your honourable master?'

> 'Friend, my Master is the Son of the Shakya House, a descendant of kings. I am a novice. I cannot tell the great heights of the law but I can give its spirit.' And after musing a moment, Assaji said (in words which have become a famous summary): 'The Awakened One teaches that the existences which appear separate are dependent upon One Cause and upon one another, and that their apparent separateness springs from ignorance and illusion as to the Cause. And that these (apparently separated) existences can be ended and the truth of Unity appear.'
>
> When Assaji said this, suddenly all the implications were clear as light before the mind of Sariputta and he knew the truth.
>
> 'There is but One Unchanging, Permanent and Eternal, of which the true Self is a part.'
>
> Deeply moved he said to Assaji: 'If the teaching were no more, it at all events makes an end to sorrow.'
>
> And he ran quickly to his friend Moggalana, who cried out: 'Your eyes shine. Have you found deliverance from death?'
>
> Sariputta answered breathlessly: 'I have found it. I have found it!' And so told him.
>
> On the great intellect of Moggalana also flashed the clear perception, and without an instant's delay they ran to the wood where the Perfect One sat in the shade surrounded by his Order.
>
> So they came and told him their cause and the Lord said: 'Come, monks, the doctrine is well taught. Lead henceforward a pure life for the extinction of sorrow.'

Stress is on living a life of purity.
Blessed are the pure in heart: for they shall see God.[7]

To be pure is to be pure in thought and action. To live, one has to work. We are born to work. Work is the greatest salvation of mankind. Without work even the maintenance of our bodies would not be possible. Body-bound as we are, our flesh and blood is commonly the mainspring of all our actions. But to get joy and fulfilment out of our work, small or great, day-to-day, mundane, one must know the secret of work. This can inevitably lead one towards the Supreme Goal – the Realization of Reality.

The secret is *Nishkama Karma*, that is, to perform right action without attachment and without hoping for the results of our actions.

> Thy business is with the action only, never with its fruits; so let not the fruit of action be thy motive nor be thou to inaction attached.[8]

> For us, there is only the trying.
> The rest is not our business.[9]

> Desire for the fruit of action denotes lack of faith in the unquestioned Master of all actions. It is an affront to the Divine.[10]

By performing action without attachment and surrendering all actions to the Supreme, leads one to the Supreme.

What is Right Action?

Right action is to act in union with the Divine. It is unselfish and detached action. It springs from right thinking. In the ultimate analysis, right action is motivated by a pure mind which is ever blessed with Divine Grace. A pure mind is like a rippleless lake, clear and transparent. It is the reflection of Reality. Pure awareness shines in it and is reflected in one's character and personality.

According to the Great Sage Vashishta, the Preceptor of Lord Rama, mind and action – *i.e.* Karma – go together as fire and heat go together. The one cannot exist without the other.

Mind is the sixth sense veiled in matter – the most powerful of all other senses. It is also the most important and powerful medium of knowledge, range and depth of which are immeasurable. Mind is the source of our actions. It can be the cause of bondage as also the key to liberation. Mind plays the most dominant role in one's life. Battles of life are primarily fought and won in man's mind. Great thoughts precede great actions. They precede war and peace, revolution and reformation. He who can control his mind, can control his destiny.

Desire, which is the projection of man's mind, is the root cause of evil and all our ills. We suffer more by desire for things than by lack of things. Greed, attachment, anger, hatred and pride are the offsprings of desire and symptoms of an impure mind.

Bernard Shaw in his inimitable way said: 'There are two tragedies in life. One is to lose your heart's desire. The other is to gain it.'[11] Desire, if fulfilled, becomes the cause of attachment and thirst for more and consequently breeds dissatisfaction. If suppressed, it produces anger and resentment calculated to cloud and confuse the mind.

The pure mind is a mind without desire. It is imbued with equanimity. It has equilibrium. It is not conscious of one's own virtues or critical of the faults and shortcomings of others. It is not susceptible to praise or blame, aversion or animosity.

A person without desire is without ego and is, therefore, without fear, envy, anger and hate. He rejoices in the welfare of all. He has no wants and, therefore, is the richest of the rich. Desirelessness is, in fact, the key to freedom and supreme peace. It is the highest bliss.

He who has acquired this awareness and reaches the state of serenity, very difficult to attain, has achieved all that he needs to achieve in life. Forgiveness, compassion, good-will towards all and self-surrender to the Divine Will are the best and surest ways to reach the state of desirelessness.

Desirelessness does not mean to work without any motivation. It does not mean that one should lose one's zest in life and act in a casual and indifferent way in carrying out the duties imposed by one's position in life. One must continue to work diligently, earnestly, wholeheartedly, but without attachment and without hankering after the fruits of action. Thus, work becomes worship – a consecration at the altar of the Divine.

It is not commonly understood and realized that the real aim of discharging one's duty diligently is not the enjoyment of transient happiness, but release from bondage of pleasure and pain which ultimately takes one towards the Realization of Reality.

I remember Krishnamurthi speaking at the Constitution Club in 1982 during his annual visit to Delhi. After his discourse, he was asked, 'You have been teaching thus for over 50 years. What have you been able to achieve?'

He replied: 'I have been lecturing not to reform you but to fulfil my own life.'

We have to put our best foot forward and Kindly Light will lead us on to the next step. This way we can get the best out of life and know and understand the joy of living. And what is more, we will be at peace.

This is the secret of right work and right action.

There remains the bewildering question of fate and free will.

How is one to explain the inequities of birth? One is born an heir to the throne and to a vast empire of wealth, the other is born in a lowly and wretched home. One is born with high intelligence and becomes a great scholar, the other is born sub-normal and dies a dithering fool. One is healthy and strong, the other is weakling and deformed. One is born in circumstances which project him as a great leader of men and the other ends his days with a begging-bowl in his hand. There are supermen, great men and men of destiny who have changed the shape of the world and laid the foundations of great dynasties and great empires. There are, on the other hand, vacillating weaklings who find it hard to make their two ends meet and end up in penury, want and wretchedness.

How is one to explain this? The just and the merciful Creator could not be responsible for perpetrating such inequities and injustices.

Of all the theories and explanations, the Doctrine of Karma, as propounded in Gita, offers a more logical explanation. The Greeks, independently of Hindu thought, also arrived at the same conclusion. As an Aryan race, the Greeks cremated their dead. They believed in the individual soul and accepted the Doctrine of Reincarnation. According to Swami Vivekananda, it was easy for the Greeks to accept this concept through the teachings of Pythagoras, who is believed to be the first Greek to teach the Theory of Palingenesis – a new or second birth into a higher or better life.

Despite all explanations and theories, Life remains a mystery wrapped in mystery. Mysterious are the ways of God and mysterious are the consequences of Karma. There are numberless causes producing numberless effects. Every moment becomes a cause which, in turn, gives rise to an effect. Every beginning has an end which, in turn, becomes a beginning. Who is to keep accounts? It is difficult for the human mind to comprehend Reality through the dense fog of Maha Maya – the Great Illusion. The tree of life is a riddle, an enigma. 'Nor here may be acquired knowledge of its form, nor its end, nor its origin, nor its rooting place.'[12]

No two days are alike. Our life hangs by a slender thread. The law of Karma can, however, be seen and discerned in one's day-to-day life. It is reflected in man's nature, in his temperament, sensitivity, self-control, balance and equanimity and in the way he reacts to situations. Our character, our personality, our make-up, our sensitivity to right and wrong, joys and sufferings, are the result of our past. To a sensitive mind, sometimes a pin-prick may have the effect of a stab wound; sometimes little obstacles and difficulties may bring about dismay and dejection, leading one to suicide or other tragic consequences. How one faces and braves life, how well or ill one lives from day to day is due to one's make-up which one has acquired in the past.

Every moment our character and destiny are being shaped by ourselves. No one escapes the consequences of one's thought and action, good or bad. Wages of sin is suffering and death. And the fruit of right action is inner joy and freedom from bondage. If one commits a crime, one may escape punishment at the hands of the law, but one cannot escape Providential justice. One will have to pay for it in suffering one way or the other. For an acquitted murderer, for example, every day will become a living death.

According to Buddhist and Hindu concepts, the doctrine of Karma is closely connected with the cycle of birth and death. What we are today is the result of our past actions. What we are going to be in future will be the result of our present thoughts and actions.

We are timeless. Consequences of our present actions may appear immediately or in a matter of days. The effect could also remain dormant for years before it surfaces. But at one time or the other, the cause must have its effect. This is the law of life.

In this world, there is a perfect balance, action and reaction being equal and opposite. In the words of Emerson, cause and effect, means and ends, seed and fruit cannot be severed, for the effect already blooms in the cause, the ends pre-exist in the means, the fruit in the seed.

Our joys and sorrows, our wealth and position, ailments of our body and mind are all the results of our Karma. One gets nothing in life which is undeserved.

Fate, free-will, Grace of God – these constitute one's life. Fate, in fact, is nothing but the Grace of the

Higher Power; but you get it only if you have deserved it. In the words of Kersy Katrak, man is a mixture of fate and free-will and it is impossible to foretell on which occasion the essential free-will of the human spirit will intervene in the fixed and fated conditioning of the past and by acting against it, alter the future.

The theory of Karma is sometimes confused with fate. This is not so. In his famous Upton Lectures of 1926, Dr Radhakrishnan lucidly explains the doctrine. In his words, we carry with us the whole past. It is an indelible record, which time cannot blur, nor death erase. At the same time, there is also free-will. The cards in the game of life are given to us. We do not select them. Although they can be traced to our past Karma, we can call as we please, lead what suit we will, and as we play, we gain or lose. And there is freedom.[13]

> Men at some time are masters of their fates:
> The fault, dear Brutus, is not in our stars.[14]

During one of my calls on Dr Radhakrishnan, then President of India, he remarked:

'What kind of ministers have you got? They make appointments with me and then cancel the same after consulting astrologers.'

'They are your ministers, not mine' was my simple reply.

'Why don't they go to the maker and breaker of all the planets,' Dr Radhakrishnan continued, 'at whose bidding anything can be achieved or altered?'

Human life is like Shakespearian tragedies, when a particular flaw in human nature, be it passion, anger, greed, attachment or pride, brings one's down-fall and destruction. But there is a Higher Will without whose aid not a sparrow chirps nor a leaf falls and before Whom impossible becomes possible and possible impossible.

One can rise above and go beyond the Laws of Karma. One can wipe out one's past and completely change one's destiny.

Meditate on Brahma. Knower of Brahma becomes Brahma. By being attuned to the Eternal, one can acquire the powers of the Eternal and thereby reach the state of singularity when all laws of cause and effect and all mathematical equations break down. All the inevitable and destined consequences of our past actions, termed as *Prarabdh*, can be wiped out. When flood comes, it washes away everything.

Chapter Fifteen

MANKIND AND THE UNIVERSE

ACCORDING TO Professor David Bohm's hypothesis which is compatible with Bell's Theorem there is basic oneness of the Universe and we cannot decompose the world into independently existing smaller units.

The basic oneness of the Universe is not only the central characteristic of mystical experience, but is also one of the most important revelations of modern physics. It becomes apparent at the atomic level and manifests itself more and more as one penetrates deeper into matter, down into the realm of sub-atomic particle.[1]

Humanity is one and there is no difference between man and man. We have the self same Source – a common heritage. That with all its diversity there is a basic oneness and unity of life and that Ultimate Reality underlines and unifies the multiplicity of things and events.

All individuals being the limbs of the same body, you cannot affect one part without affecting the whole. It is one world. In fact, it is one Universe. 'You cannot stir a flower without disturbing a star.'[2]

This is the basic and universal law which unifies humanity. This is the basic and universal law which unifies Space and Time. It governs the Universe, with its galaxies of stars, of worlds beyond worlds.

The human mind is part of the Master Mind. The

human heart beats with the rhythm of the Whole, of which Love is its greatest manifestation.

Love is the greatest religion. There is no creed higher than Love. Love is God. He manifests Himself as Love in all mankind. 'Man all over the world is alike in his basic emotions and feelings, for his true nature is nothing else but Love.'[3]

Joy flows from Love. Where there is sorrow, there cannot be Love. Love, says Krishnamurti, is not an emotion or a sentiment. It is tremendously vital – as strong as Death. Without Love there are no fellow feelings, no compassion. Without Love, life has little or no meaning. It is the fundamental Beauty of life.[4]

Love generates and regenerates feelings of peace, goodwill and happiness. He prayeth best who loveth best.[5] There is no greater prayer than to send waves of Love in all the four directions.

Love is its own fulfilment. One who radiates love is blessed by his own radiance.

Love is the basic urge and emotion behind the First Cause. It is a many-splendoured thing. It supports heaven and earth. It makes the sun shine, the stars twinkle and the moon wax and wane. Because of it, the earth revolves and the day follows the night, the rivers flow, the oceans heave, the rain comes and rainbow colours the sky.

It is the Eternal Law which gives life and sustains it on earth. It gives grace and glow and order to our existence and an awareness to our consciousness of wonder, power and glory. The whole cosmos vibrates with its rhythmn. Love is Truth, Beauty and Goodness. It is Peace. It is Bliss. It is man's salvation.[6]

It is on the basic principle of Oneness of mankind and Love that the fabric of the world is woven. Enlightened philosophy, ethics of good governance, progressive and successful policies and pursuits in business or any other profession are based on this basic principle. You cannot ever go wrong in following this Fundamental Law. This is the secret of success and fulfilment of life. Most men discover this by trial and error. Only judicious men, men of insight and imagination, men with understanding of the intrinsic and eternal human values follow this straight and narrow path and in the process bring joy, happiness and contentment not only to themselves but to the whole community and nation.

This is not just utopian thinking, but the law of life. The good of the individual is contained in the good of the community, the good of the community in the good of the State or nation and the good of the nation is contained in the good of the world and the largest interest of mankind as a whole.

In other words, on closer analysis, with progressive and enlightened thinking as guide, one discovers that there cannot be a conflict between national interests and interests of world peace.

Foreign policy of any government, removed from this basic principle and divorced from the consideration of larger interests of mankind, of peace of the region and the world, must create problems, run into difficulties and eventually, after a period of time, fail.

The same is true of internal politics and policies of a party or government. Administration of a district or a State or a country divorced from uniformity of justice and considerations of the good of the common man, must have ugly repercussions and an ugly end. Such indifferent or selfish approach must eventually recoil on those responsible for the perpetration of inequalities and injustices and affect not only them but their children and children's children. A good administrator, a good business executive, a good Governor, Prime Minister or President, has therefore, to avoid at all costs any temptations, however great, for selfish or political gain or end which deflects from the great and noble path of integrity, honesty and uniformity of justice.

The Universe is the embodiment of the Mystic Law which pervades all existence, says Ikeda.[7] Every individual is part of the whole. His thoughts, words and deeds, good or bad, not only affects him and his close associates and environs, but the whole world. It is just like the circles in a pond when a pebble is thrown into it. There is a circle after a circle, widening, enlarging till it reaches the farthest end. 'Those who live nobly, even if in their day they live obscurely, need not fear that they will have lived in vain. Something radiates from their lives, some light that shows the way to their friends, their neighbours, perhaps to long future ages... The individual if he is filled with love of mankind, with breadth of vision, with courage and with endurance, can do a great deal.'[8]

One good thought, thought out in the darkest cave of Himalayas, must have its effects. It is only a question of time. Lord Buddha died with only a very few disciples around him. But what he thought and preached spread throughout the length and breadth of Asia. Ajanta,

Stupas and all the Buddhist architectural grandeur which came into existence hundreds of years later, are only symbols of the glory of the mind, thought and heart of Buddha who has been deified and worshipped as a God.

Christianity only came to life three hundred years after Christ was crucified.

Same with Ramakrishna, who died amongst a few of his followers living a life of simplicity and poverty. But his message of Eternal Verities lives and keeps on widening in ever increasing circles.

Mahatma Gandhi was not an orator, but when he spoke, he moved millions of people. His words, unlike the words of hollow men, did not sound hollow. It is because he practised what he preached. His life was a beautiful poem, a noble life of high thinking, of simplicity and sacrifice. To him, the interests of mankind came before his own interests. He suffered so that others may live a life of dignity and freedom. His love had no bounds. His message of truth and non-violence and freedom found its way to the hearts of millions and millions of men and women, who looked upon him as a Messiah and the coming generation of men will worship him as god.

Bad thoughts, like good thoughts, also affect the whole. But it must be remembered that any thought or action, based on selfish considerations or for sordid ends, must have a sordid ending. Have no doubt about it. To quote Emerson, you cannot do wrong without suffering wrong. The thief steals from himself. The swindler swindles himself.

In the good of an individual lies the good of all.

Sarvodaya – Love and Compassion towards all – is an ancient Indian ethic enshrined in the common man's ritual to be lived in day-to-day life.

Satyameva Jayate – Truth alone triumphs – is a sacred Vedic ideal enshrined in the national Seal of India – a basic principle upon which rests the foundation of beings and of nations.

The twin ideals of Love and Truth need to be enshrined in the hearts and minds of every man, but most of all those who have responsibility for the good governance of a country and for the peace of the world. To redeem the human race of its ills, philosophers have to become kings and kings philosophers and live high philosophy.

Therein may lie the salvation of mankind.

SONG OF CREATION[1]

When the morning stars sang together and all the sons of God shouted for joy

Job 38.7

I

THERE WAS neither being nor non-being
There was no sky, no heaven beyond the sky
No Sun, no earth or ether
No light but darkness folded in darkness.
Was there an abyss of fathomless Waters?
A fluid and formless mass?
A point of Infinite Density
In which time and space merged as one.
The race of time had yet to run.

Who knows
Whence comes this creation
There was neither day nor night
Nor death nor immortality
Who can tell whence and how arose the Universe?

The gods are later than its beginning
And later came the man – the Crown of Creation
With trains of prophets and priests
Seers and saints
And saviours of mankind.

II

In the beginning was the One,
The Void and the Word.
What power was there? Where?
Who was that power?
The One was brooding over the Self
Breathing by its own power in deep peace
Only the One was – there was nothing beyond.

In the One
Arose Kalpana[2] – fire of fervour.
It was the dawn of Love:
Its rays spread above, below and sideways.
Love, the first seed of Soul,
The truth of it the sages found in their hearts;
Seeking in their hearts with wisdom
The sages found that bond of union
Between being and non-being.

With Love came Joy, Bliss and Beatitude.
The Whole Creation is conceived in Love,
Hath its being in Love,
And in Love dissolves.

III

Steeped in Love and Bliss
The One projected Himself and multiplied.
Who was the Witness?
Who is to describe the moment of Creation
When Primal Energy forth-streamed
And like rays the Universe was spread
When suns and moons and stars
Appeared in their newly-created heavens
And Worlds upon Worlds,
Worlds beyond Worlds rolled out?

How to describe the moment of creation?
The vision of marvels
The forth-streaming Cosmic Force –
Without source or midst or end
Vast, immeasurable, beyond words –
Projected mountains and unbounded forms,
Fiery firmaments, typhoons and turbulent seas
A shining mass of splendour, everywhere,
Like the splendour of a thousand suns
Blazing out together in the sky.

IV

O! the joy of creation,
The glory and the grandeur,
The song and the splendour.

There was light,
There was sun and air,
Blue skies and seas,
Earth and æther, hills and dales,
Earth – a paradise of many-coloured hues
With music of the spheres vibrating
Rhythms eternal of Beauty, Love and Bliss

The Sun, the moon and the stars
And Countless other orbs
In their appointed Courses bound,
And all other created things,
Moving and Unmoving
Sang the Song of Creation
A symphony of adoration and love
Praising their Maker.

V

In the beginning was the One,
The Void and the Word
Brooding over Silence of Its own,
The One without a Second,
The One from whence
The Ancient Energy forth-streamed.

First Cause – First of the Gods,
Father of the Worlds,
Of all that moves and stands,
Supreme Solace of all that lives –
He is the Self of all;
All evolve from One
And into One all dissolve.

He is the beginning, the middle
And the end of creation,
The Origin of all to come.
He is everlasting Time,
The Creation and the Dissolution,
The Resurrection and the Life.
His Will is Law,
His shadow is death,
His touch immortality.

Self effulgent – Light of all lights,
Which lightens the suns and the stars
The One Eternal, Spirit Supreme,
With one fragment of Himself
Pervades the Universe
And all His Creation.

Satyam, Gyanam, Anantam Brahma
Shantam, Shivam, Sundaram Brahma
Anand roopam, Ekam Brahma
Ekam Eva, Advaitam Brahma.[3]

Chapter Sixteen

MY SONG

EVERY LIFE IS A POEM, often recited but seldom sung. And, more often than not, it is neither recited nor sung but interned with the individual.

What is the usual burden of one's song? And how well the singer sang the song of his life?

The common song of the average individual is the usual song of humanity – the song of loves and hates, of rights and wrongs, of sickness, suffering and sorrow, with brief, very brief, interludes of sighs of relief, of fading pleasures, of fleeting joys. It is often the song of wistful longing, of hopes belied, of dreams unfulfilled.

I too have a song to sing. Like everyone else, I have been through many a vicissitude of life and had my share of suffering which seemed much more poignant than most by virtue of my being of an over-sensitive nature. But I have the satisfaction of living a full life. I have made mistakes but I have not done anything of which I feel ashamed. I have tried to live through life gracefully and aesthetically, relishing both its lights and its shadows. I have, so far as is humanly possible, tried to take the straight and narrow path. It is a harder and more difficult approach to life but in the long run it is self-fulfilling.

Life, with all its various complexities, is not only a challenge but also a series of experiences. It is also an eternal struggle between good and evil. And I have always fought against injustice for which very often I have come to grief. In life good suffers along with evil, but in the long run good triumphs and in the process one goes up in self-esteem and stature. Even your worst detractors develop sneaking respect and regard for you.

Three things carried me through life. Faith in myself and my destiny, faith in the Protecting Providence and, what is more, faith in the inherent goodness of human nature. This firm and unshakeable faith has given a meaning and direction to my existence.

I discovered, not without trial and error, that human nature responds to goodness, kindness and love. The difference between a great man and a small man, a good administrator and a bad administrator, is that the former brings out the best in you while the latter brings out the worst. It is given to men like Gandhiji who made saints out of sinners and through sufferings and self-discipline, gave self-respect and dignity to the lowly and the lost, inculcating high ideals of purity, truth and justice.

All along Inscrutable High Intelligence seems to have been my guide. I cannot be too grateful for the Providential blessings. By His Grace abounding, I have had interludes of serenity and peace which surpasseth all understanding.

Although possessing an average intelligence, I have been fortunate to be blessed with God-given urge and inspiration to know and to understand, which enabled me to contemplate and probe into the sweet mystery of life and the strange mystery of death which surround us. What is the purpose and goal of life? Who am I?

Where did I come from? Why do I exist? Where am I going to? The questions and their attempted answers form the burden of my present work. It has been fascinating indeed to ponder over man's life, his destiny and finally its fulfilment. In the process I have been reading, writing, learning and growing. There are new vistas, new horizons, beyond the bounds of thought and it is a unique experience indeed to be centred in the Self and contemplate the vast dimensions of Truth and Reality.

Like most others, my life has been a long quest for peace and happiness. But peace I did not find in wealth, in position or in power, which, in this graded world of high and low, are only comparative. I have come to discover that happiness can often be found in small things. Little courtesies, a smile, a pleasant gesture, a word of comfort go a long way to bring more sunshine in this world of chequered shade. That an effort to relieve the headache of others, somehow, helps to relieve one's own.

I found life an endless unfolding and an endless process of self-discovery. The aim and purpose of life, I discovered, is not mere acquisition of wealth and property, power and position or even name and fame. These are pursuits of an average and common mind and in the ultimate analysis a measure of mediocrity. It is the quality you give to your life and mind that matters. The important thing in life is not what you have been but what you are reaching for and becoming.

At my age when I can see the end of the road more clearly than most, I find that life is far too short and feel as if time is flying. When I sit back and recollect in tranquillity the varying vicissitudes of my life and what it has taught me, I find that the great and glorious hours of my life were those when I gave a helping hand to others without expecting anything in return and not when I struggled and succeeded in gaining my selfish ends. And I can well imagine and appreciate that in this world those alone live who live for others. I have no regrets for the past. Life on the whole has been comparatively kind to me. My only regret is that I received more from life than I gave.

I am becoming convinced that life begins at 70.

> Grow old along with me!
> The best is yet to be,
> The last of life, for which the first was made.[1]

Old age is a result of the obsession of our mind which affects us mentally and physically. We are all bits of the sun and have similar self-renewing energy which we can exercise if only we were to contemplate and discover it.

I have come to realize that life without direction and motivation is a prescription for old age and a living death. And that basically man's salvation lies through work. Since I retired from the Diplomatic Service in 1973, I have not known a single dull moment. I am never lonely when alone. I do not know what boredom is – a grey area which, on the diversely coloured canvas of life, is a common malady that at one time or the other can afflict all individuals. And it normally afflicts those who have ceased to think and to value time; who have lost the sense of wonder and can no longer see the beauty around and feel the spirit that pervades the core of our being.

There can be nothing more satisfying and becoming

in life than to drop down while still in harness. Norman Cousins, the American writer and publisher has beautifully stated that death is not the greatest loss in life. The greatest loss is what dies inside us while we live. And I have tried not to allow this to happen to me.

The art of growing old gracefully, like any other art, does not come so easily. A lifetime of dedication, discipline, right thinking and right living is necessary. The greatest wisdom is to know the highest truth and to live in harmony with it. There is peace and tranquillity in living a simple life of high idealism and low profile. To put it in Bertrand Russell's words:

'Those who live nobly, even if in their days they live obscurely, need not fear that they will have lived in vain. Something radiates from their lives, some light that shows the way to their friends, their neighbours, perhaps to long future ages'.[2]

The human nature with all its failings and shortcomings has not changed much since the days of Mahabharata and is likely to remain so. The age old conflicts will continue till realization dawns that there is no confusion in the world; the confusion is in our own minds. It is one's approach to life and contact and relationship with the world that matters. It can be a wasteful confrontation or constructive cooperation; ending up either in tragic conflicts and consequences or in a progressive, fruitful and harmonious haven of peace.

I can visualize and cover my life span in less than an hour. At my age – now well over 80 – the panorama of the past looks like a dream, a passing show, an airy nothing. It is like a film show. And I can sit back and watch as a detached spectator and muse and wonder at man's nature and his pursuits, the pitfalls of life and the follies of humankind. The show is not quite over and, though coming to a close, it continues to retain some interest and a hope that it does not end up with a whimper.

EPILOGUE

Here ends the Song of my Life. My work is done. It has been self-fulfilling. And now I join my thoughts with Walter Savage Landor:

> I strove with none; for none was worth my strife;
>   Nature I loved, and, next to Nature, Art;
> I warmed both hands before the fire of life;
>   It sinks, and I am ready to depart.

The innermost urge of my life still remains. This may perhaps be expressed in what I would like to have as my Epitaph:

Maha Shunya

This world is no home
'Tis a wilderness.
Nothing do I own,
Nothing do I call my own.
Desireless, drunk with the Joy of Life
I dwell in Nothingness
In the Great Void
Where Silence Reigns.

NOTES

MY QUEST FOR THE ETERNAL

1. All is verily Brahma.
2. Preface to Dr Alexander Lipski: *Life and Teachings of Shree Anandamayee Ma*.
3. Friedrich Max Muller.

PROLOGUE

1. Extract from Author's letter of 1 January 1987, to Mr T. N. Kaul, then India's Ambassador to the USSR.
2. Extract from Author's letter of 27 September 1986, to Mr Rajiv Gandhi, then Prime Minister of India.

IN THE BEGINNING

1. In 1929 Hubble showed that the Universe is expanding. Stephen W. Hawking calls this discovery 'one of the intellectual revolutions of the twentieth century'.
2. The word 'before' is used in relation to 'imaginary' time. There was no 'before' as 'real' time began and 'real' space, as distinct from 'imaginary' space (whatever that may mean), came into existence with the Big Bang.
3. Timothy Ferris, author of *Galaxies,* in his article 'The Frontiers of Physics'.
4. Fritjof Capra: *The Tao of Physics,* Chapter 14, 'Emptiness and Form'.
5. Virtual particle: In quantum mechanics, a particle that can never be directly detected, but whose existence does have measurable effects. – Stephen W. Hawking: *A Brief History of Time,* Chapter 5.

6. Fritjof Capra: *The Tao of Physics,* Chapter 14 'Emptiness and Form'.
7. Hegel: *The Universe and Dr Einstein.*
8. At the Big Crunch Matter will turn into Energy as, at the time of the Big Bang, Energy converted into Matter. According to Professor Hawking in *A Brief History of Time* the total Energy of the Universe is exactly Zero.
9. Lama Anagarika Govinda: *Creative Meditation and Multi-dimensional Consciousness.*
10. *Chandogya Upanishad* 4.x.4.

THE FUNDAMENTAL FORCE

1. Hegel: *The Universe and Dr Einstein.*
2. John Boslough: *Stephen Hawking's Universe.*
3. *Ibid.*
4. Einstein's famous equation: $E=mc^2$ (c being the speed of light). This led to such advances as the harnessing of nuclear power.
5. Quoted by Guy Murchie in *The Seven Mysteries of Life.*

THE NATURE OF REALITY

1. Sanskrit translation by Robert Ernest Hume: *The Thirteen Principle Upanishads.*
2. *Prana Upanishad* 6.4; *Mundaka Upanishad* 2.1.3; *Chandogya Upanishad* 4.10.4.
3. Quoted by Rudy Rucker: *Infinity and the Mind, The Science and Philosophy of the Infinite.*
4. *Svestasvatara Upanishad* 4.20.
5. *Mundaka Upanishad* 2.2.10. *Katha Upanishad* 5.15. *Svestasvatara Upanishad* 6.14

   'The sun shines not there, nor the moon and stars
   These lightnings shine not, much less this (earthly) fire!
   After Him, as He shines, doth everything shine,
   This whole world is illuminated with His light.'

6. *Bhagavad Gita,* 11.12.
7. *Ibid.* 13-15, 16, 17.
8. *Ibid.*
9. '*Sat-Asat*': Being and non-being. (The final pair of opposites, beyond which is only the One.)
10. *Bhagavad Gita,* 13.14.
11. *Ibid.* 10.41.
12. To see a World in a Grain of Sand
    And a Heaven in a Wild flower,
    Hold Infinity in the palm of your hand,
    And Eternity in an hour. –
    William Blake: *Auguries of Innocence.*
13. Fritjof Capra: *The Tao of Physics.*
14. *Mundaka Upanishad* 1.1.7.
15. W. B. Yeats: *The Tower.*
16. Daisaku Ikeda: *Life – An Enigma, a Precious Jewel.*

THE BIRTH OF RELIGION

1. Some of the hymns of Rig Veda are supposed to have beenconceived in Balkh (Afghanistan) which I visited during my posting at Kabul (1960–64). A serenity pervades the atmosphere and the vibrations of ages past still seem to linger in the surrounding vastness.
2. *The Book of Job,* 14.1.
3. Wisdom of Hinduism, quoted by Mrs Vijaylakshmi Pandit in *The Scope of Happiness.*
4. 'Life is Suffering', an article by James Reston in *Bangkok World* of 7 June 1973.
5. *St Matthew* 11.28.
6. *Ibid.* 28.20.
7. Swami Sharnananda.

SCIENCE AND RELIGION

1. Fritjof Capra: *The Turning Point,* Chapter 9, 'The System's View of Life'.
2. See Paul Davies: *God and the New Physics* (quoted by Michael Talbot in *Beyond the Quantum World*, Chapter on 'Mathematical Evidence of the Existence of God').
3. 'Equations are more important to me, because politics is for the present, but an equation is something for Eternity.' – Albert Einstein.
4. 'Biographical Sketch of Galileo Galilei' in Stephen W. Hawking: *A Brief History of Time.*
5. Frederick Coplaston: *History of Philosophy*, Vol. IV, Chapter VI.
6. *Ibid.* Vol. IV.
7. Quoted by Gary Zukav: *The Dancing Wu Li Masters.*
8. Stephen W. Hawking: *A Brief History of Time.*

PHYSICS AND METAPHYSICS

1. Stephen W. Hawking's Inaugural Lecture: 'Is the End in Sight for Theoretical Physics?' reproduced as Appendix by John Boslough in *Stephen Hawking's Universe.*
2. Stephen W. Hawking: *A Brief History of Time.*
3. Gary Zukav: *The Dancing Wu Li Masters.*
4. Albert Einstein: 'On Physical Reality', Franklin Institute Journals.
5. Stapp (1971) as quoted by Fritjof Capra in *The Turning Point.*
6. Stephen W. Hawking: *A Brief History of Time.*
7. *The Dancing Wu Li Masters,* 'The End of Science'.
8. Gary Zukav: *The Dancing Wu Li Masters*: 'The End of Science'.
9. *Ibid.*
10. Michael Talbot: *Beyond The Quantum World.*
11. J. Krishnamurti and David Bohm: *The Ending of Time.*

12. Gary Zukav: *The Dancing Wu Li Masters,* 'The End of Science'.
13. Sir Fred Hoyle: *Intelligent Universe,* as quoted by Michael Talbot in *Beyond the Quantum World.*
14. Paul Davies: *God and the New Physics,* as quoted by Michael Talbot in *Beyond the Quantum World.*
15. Lord Orrery's Theorem says: 'If the model of any natural system requires intelligence for its creation and its working, the real natural system requires at least as much intelligence for its own creation and working.'
16. David Bohm, as quoted by Gary Zukav in *The Dancing Wu Li Masters.*
17 Quoted by Guy Murchie: *The Seven Mysteries of Life.*
18. *Ibid.*
19. Stephen W. Hawking: *A Brief History of Time.*

MIND, THOUGHT AND MAYA

1. Gary Zukav: *The Dancing Wu Li Masters.*
2. *Ibid.*
3. Stephen W. Hawking's Inaugural Lecture: 'Is the End in Sight for Theoretical Physics?' reproduced as Appendix by John Boslough in *Stephen Hawking's Universe.*
4. *Span* of June 1991.
5. P. B. Shelley: *Prometheus Unbound.*

   'He gave man speech, and speech created thought,
   Which is the measure of the Universe.'
6. Works of Swami Vivekananda, Vol. II.
7. Rudy Rucker: *Infinity and the Mind, The Science and Philosophy of the Infinite.*
8. Guy Murchie: *Music of the Spheres,* Vol. II.
9. Black Holes are black voids in space, regions of space-time from which nothing, not even light can escape, because their gravity is so strong. (see A *Brief History of Time,* Chapters VI and VII).
10. Rudy Rucker: *Infinity and the Mind.*

11. L. Adams Beck: *The Story of Oriental Philosophy.*
12. Gary Zukav: *The Dancing Wu Li Masters*– Chapter on 'End of Science'.
13. Karan Singh and Daisaku Ideda: *Humanity at the Crossroads.*
14. Sir James Jeans (1930) quoted in *The Turning Point*.
15. Gary Zukav: *The Dancing Wu Li Masters.*
16. John Boslough: *Stephen Hawking's Universe.*
17. H. W. Longfellow: *A Psalm of Life.*
18. *The Book of Ecclesiasticus.*
19. P. B. Shelley: *Adonais.*
20. These are common examples given by almost all texts on the subject to illustrate the basic point.
21. Walter Sullivan in the *New York Times.* Reproduced in the *Reader's Digest* of September 1972.
22. *The Gospel Of Sri Ramakrishna*.
23. Arnold J. Toynbee: *Surviving the Future.*
24. William H. McNeill: *Arnold J. Toynbee, A Life.*
25. What is this life if, full of care,
    We have no time to stand and stare? –
    W. H. Davies.
26. All this is verily Brahma.

CONSCIOUSNESS AND THE COSMOS

1. The *Devi-Mahatmyam*, called *Durga Saptasati* or the *Chandi*, like the *Gita*, is the sacred text of Hindus for daily reading or reciting. It forms part of *Markandeya Purana*.
2. Fritjof Capra: *The Turning Point*.
3. Samuel Taylor Coleridge: *Dejection, An Ode.*
4. Fritjof Capra: *The Turning Point*.
5. Michael Talbot: *Beyond the Quantum World,* Chapter IV – 'What and Where is Consciousness?'
6. *Brihad-Aranyaka Upanishad* 4.2.2, 4.5.15.
7. See *Mundaka Upanishad* – 2.1.3.
8. Big Crunch means the singularity at the end of the Universe
9. Stephen W. Hawking: *A Brief History of Time*. The word

'zero' when translated into Sanskrit is Shunya. Shunya is also the Primordial Void of the Eastern mystics.

10. Fritjof Capra: *The Turning Point*.
11. David Bohm: *Wholeness And The Implicate Order.*
12. Sri Nisargadatta Maharaj: *I Am That*.
13. Michael Talbot: *Beyond the Quantum World.*
14. *Ibid.*
15. *Ibid.*
16. *Ibid.*
17. *Aitareya Upanishad* 3.5.
18. *Mundaka Upanishad* 2.2.5.
19. *Brihad-Aranyaka Upanishad* 3.7.23.
20. *Kena Upanishad* 1.2.
21. Peper: *An Historian's Conscience*, letter A. J. Toynbee to Columbia, 25 January 1972.
22. Paul Davies: *God and the New Physics*.
23. *Gita* 15.7 and 15.8.
24. See the *Bhagavadgita* by Radhakrishnan – Commentary on Sloka 15.7.
25. *Mundaka Upanishad* – 3.2.8.
26. *Gita* 13.17.
27. Sri Nisargadatta Maharaj: *I Am That*.
28. Sankaracharya: *Viveka-Chudamani*, Verse 3.
29. John Wheeler: *The Mystery and Message of the Quantum.* Lecture given to the American Physical Society – 1 February 1984. Quoted by Michael Talbot: *Beyond the Quantum World.*
30. Sri Nisargadatta Maharaj: *I Am That*.
31. *Gita* 2.23.
32. Sri Nisargadatta Maharaj: *I Am That*.
33. *Gita* 2.13.
34. Sri Nisargadatta Maharaj: *I Am That*.
35. *Ibid.*
36. Bertrand Russell: *New Hope for a Changing World,* Chapter XX: 'The Happy Man'.
37. Sir Edwin Arnold: *Light of Asia*.

ON CONSCIOUSNESS

1. *The Complete Works of Swami Vivekananda* Vol. III.
2. *Katha Upanishad*, 6.2.
3. *Prana Upanishad*, 2.6.
4. Sri Nisargadatta Maharaj: *I Am That.*
5. *The Complete Works of Swami Vivekananda*, Vol. I.
6. *Kaushitaki Upanishad.*
7. *Ibid.* 2.1.
8. *The Complete Works of Swami Vivekananda* Vol. I.
9. Acquisition of knowledge and wisdom.
10. Prayers, Meditation and Worship.
11. Conduct and action.
12. *Vide* Joint Paper by Stephen W. Hawking and Roger Penrose in 1970.
13. See Article by Michael D. Lemonick in *Time International* of 4 May 1992.
14. *Rig Veda,* 10th Mandala, 129.
15. Kurt Gödel (1906-78): Well known Austrian-born American logician and mathematician of Gödel's Theorem (1931) fame.
16. Quoted by Rudy Rucker in *Infinity and the Mind.*
17. *Aitareya Upanishad* (*Rig Veda*).
18. William Shakespeare: *The Merchant of Venice.*
19. *Himalayas*: Preface by Arnold Toynbee (His Impressions during his journey by air from Rawalpindi to Gilgit).
20. Brahma – the One
Only the One Without a second,
Beauty, Truth, Goodness
Knowledge, Peace, Infinitude
Pure Consciousness and Bliss.
21. John Boslough: *The Riddle of Time,* (as condensed from *National Geographic* in *Reader's Digest* of June 1991).
22. Guy Murchie: *Music of the Spheres,* Vol. II.
23. *Ibid.*
24. T. S. Eliot: *Burnt Norton.*

25. T. S. Eliot: *The Dry Salvages.*
26. T. S. Eliot: *Burnt Norton.*
27. J. Krishnamurti: *Poems and Parables.*
28. 'Whoever knows the Eternal becomes the Eternal'
– Anquetil Duperron.
29 Sri Nisargadatta Maharaj: *I Am That.*
30 *Ibid.*
31 *Ibid.*
32. *Gita* XII.12.
33. Sri Nisargadatta Maharaj: *I Am That.*
34. P. B. Shelley.
35. *The Complete Works of Swami Vivekananda* Vol. III.
36. *Chandogya Upanishad – Sama Veda.*
37. *Brihadaranyaka Upanishad – Yajur Veda.*
38. *Mandukya Upanishad – Atharva Veda.*
39. *Aitareya Upanishad – Rig Veda.*
40. *St John* 10:30.
41. Quoted by H. McNeill in *Arnold J. Toynbee: A Life.*
42. Michael Talbot: *Beyond the Quantum World,* Chapter VII.
43. *Brihad-Aranyaka Upanishad* – 3.8.9.
44. To see a World in a Grain of Sand,
And a Heaven in a Wild Flower,
Hold Infinity in the palm of your hand,
And Eternity in an hour –
William Blake: *Auguries of Innocence.*
45. *Kaivalya Upanishad.*

THE THEORY OF RELATIVITY – I

1. Stephen W. Hawking: *A Brief History of Time.*
2. Fritjof Capra: *The Tao of Physics.*

THE THEORY OF RELATIVITY – II

1. When a positron (a positively charged particle) and an electron (an elementary particle with a negative charge that orbits the nucleus of an atom) collide they annihilate each other. What remains is energy in the form of electromagnetic radiation called photons – a particle or a quantum of light.
2. Albert Michelson, Professor of Physics at Chicago from 1892, became in 1907 the first American scientist to win the Nobel Prize. He is chiefly remembered for the Michelson-Morley experiment (1887) to determine ether drift, the negative result of which set Albert Einstein on the road to the Theory of Relativity.
3. One light-year equals the distance that a ray of light travels in the course of one year at the speed of 300,000km per second.
4. L. Landau Yu. Rumer: *What is the Theory of Relativity.*
5. Sir Isaac Newton: *Philosophiæ Naturalis Principia Mathematica (1687).*
6. Bertrand Russell: *ABC of Relativity.*
7. Harald Fritzsch: *An Equation That Changed The World.*
8. *Ibid.*
9. *Ibid.*

THE THEORY OF RELATIVITY – III

1. Stephen W. Hawking: *Black Holes and Baby Universes.*
2. Stephen W. Hawking: *A Brief History of Time.*
3. *The Epistle of Paul the Apostle to the Hebrews.*
4. *St Matthew* 28:20.
5. 'Science… means unresting endeavour and continually progressing development toward an aim which the poetic intuition may apprehend, but which the intellect can never fully grasp' – Max Planck, *The Philosophy of Physics.* (Quoted by Gary Zukav in *The Dancing Wu Li Masters.*)

6. E. P. Wigner: *Symmetries and Reflections* – Scientific Essays. (Quoted by Fritjof Capra in *The Tao of Physics.*)
7. From the *New York Times,* 19 April 1955.
8. W. H. Auden.
9. Stephen W. Hawking: *Black Holes and Baby Universes.*
10. Harald Fritzsch: *An Equation That Changed The World.*
11. From an article by Ananda Wood in the *Times of India,* 12 October 1996.
12. Ronald W. Clark: *Einstein, The Life and Times.*
13. *Ibid.*
14. Albert Einstein: *Ideas and Opinions.*
15. Gary Zukav: *The Dancing Wu Li Masters.*
16. *Tat Twam Asi: Chandogya Upanishad – Sama Veda.*
17. *The Book of Exodus* 3:14.
18. Michael White and John Gribbin: *Stephen Hawking, A Life in Science.*

THE END OF PHYSICS AND PHILOSOPHY

1. 'It is not quite correct to translate the Sanskrit word *Dharma* into English as religion or sacred duty. *Dharma* is derived from the root "dhri", meaning to hold or retain. *Dharma* is what keeps men together. It is the property of fire to burn, that of man to practice *Dharma.*' – *The Statesman,* Editorial: 20 September 1993.
2. Rudy Rucker: *Infinity and the Mind.*
3. Stephen W. Hawking's Inaugural Lecture: 'Is the End in Sight for Theoretical Physics?' reproduced as Appendix by John Boslough in *Stephen Hawking's Universe.*
4. Rudy Rucker: *Infinity And the Mind.*
5. Alfred, Lord Tennyson: *In Memoriam.*
6. The Ideas of Henry Luce, as quoted by William H. McNeill in his book *Arnold J. Toynbee: A Life.*
7. Dr Chaim Tschernowitz, as quoted by Ronald W. Clark in *Einstein: The Life and Times.*
8. Author's Journal: New Delhi, 28 January 1983.

THE REALIZATION OF REALITY

1. Article appeared in *Bangkok World* of 9 June 1973.
2. 'Seek, and ye shall find; knock, and it shall be opened unto you.' *St Matthew* 7.7.
3. W. Wordsworth: *Laodamia*.
4. *St Matthew* 9.23.
5. *Gita* 17.3.
6. L. Adams Beck: *The Story of Oriental Philosophy*, Chapter XII
7. *St Matthew* 5.3.
8. *Gita* 2:47.
9. T. S. Eliot: 'East Coker' – *Four Quartets.*
10. Swami Sharnananda.
11. G. B. Shaw: *Man and Superman.* Interestingly, Oscar Wilde came to the same conclusion in *Lady Windermere's Fan*: 'In this world there are only two tragedies. One is not getting what one wants, and the other is getting it. The last is much the worst; the last is a real tragedy.'
12. *Gita* 15.3.
13. Dr S. Radhakrishnan: *The Hindu View of Life*.
14. William Shakespeare: *Julius Caesar.*

MANKIND AND THE UNIVERSE

1. Fritjof Capra: *The Tao of Physics.*
2. Address by Mrs Indira Gandhi during Inaugural Session of the Seventh Non-Aligned Summit, on 7 March 1983.
3. Maj. R. G. Salvi: *Whom Enemies Sheltered.*
4. Heard during Krishnamurti's discourse in New Delhi on 7 November 1982 and noted in Author's Journal.
5. He prayeth well, who loveth well
   Both man and bird and beast.
   He prayeth best, who loveth best
   All things both great and small;

For the dear God who loveth us,
He made and loveth all. –
S. T. Coleridge: *The Rime of the Ancient Mariner.*

6. Author's Journal.
7. Daisaku Ikeda: *Life – An Enigma, a Precious Jewel.*
8. Bertrand Russell: *New Hopes for a Changing World.*

SONG OF CREATION

1. For this effort I owe my inspiration to the Verses of Rig Veda (10th Mandala 129) as translated by Juan Mascaro. Not least, I am indebted to the *Upanishads* and *Gita*. This poem has been vibrating within me for nearly three months. It was completed at 8.00am on Tuesday 15 January 1985 in Room 306. A.I.I.M.S. Hospital, New Delhi.
2. Kalpana: Desire, urge, will; imagination; fancy
3. Brahma – the One
   Only the One Without a second
   Beauty, Truth, Goodness
   Knowledge Peace, Infinitude
   Pure Consciousness and Bliss.

MY SONG

1. Robert Browning: *Rabbi ben Ezra.*
2. Bertrand Russell: *New Hopes for a Changing World.*

ACKNOWLEDGEMENTS

My grateful thanks are due to Derek Brewer, Emeritus Professor, whose interest, advice and intellectual support greatly helped in the publication of this book.

I thank Dharma Vira, our most senior living civil servant and administrator for his helpful and positive reactions on very carefully going through the manuscript.

My very many thanks are due to my distinguished colleague Ambassador Khub Chand, ICS, for meticulously and critically examining the manuscript.

My special thanks to Andrew Best, Literary Consultant, for his efforts in handling the manuscript and for making some useful editorial suggestions, and to David Colvin for preparing the proofs.

And lastly, I thank my staff, especially D. Vishwanathan who typed earlier portions of the manuscript and more especially my Secretary S. C. Gupta who helped to complete it.

The publishers and I are grateful for being allowed to quote brief excerpts from 'Burnt Norton', 'East Coker' and 'The Dry Salvages' in *Four Quartets,* copyright 1943 by T. S. Eliot and renewed 1971 by Esmé Valerie Eliot, printed by kind permission of Harcourt Brace & Company, and of Faber and Faber Ltd. as the publishers of *Collected Poems, 1909–1962* by T. S. Eliot.

Quotations are attributed in the text or in the Notes. Where no attribution is given, the quotation is from my own poems.

J.N.D. 1998

SELECT BIBLIOGRAPHY

Sir Edwin Arnold: *The Light of Asia*
Isaac Asimov: *The Exploding Suns*
L. Adams Beck (E. Barrington): *The Story of Oriental Philosophy*
Annie Besant: *The Bhagwat Gita*
David Bohm: *Wholeness and the Implicate Order*
John Boslough: *Stephen Hawking's Universe*
Paul Brunton:
The Inner Reality
The Quest of the Oversoul
The Hidden Teaching Beyond Yoga
Fritjof Capra:
The Tao of Physics
The Turning Point
Uncommon Wisdom
Thomas Carlyle: *Heroes and Hero-Worship*
Paul Carus: *The Gospel of Buddha*
Ronald W. Clark: *Einstein – The Life and Times*
Frederick Copleston, S. J.: *A History of Philosophy*
T. S. Eliot:
Four Quartets
Collected Poems 1909–1935
Ralph Waldo Emerson: *Essays*
Harald Fritzsch: *An Equation That Changed the World*
Lama Anagarika Govinda: *Creative Meditation & Multi-Dimensional Consciousness*
Michael White & John Gribbin: *Stephen Hawking – A Life in Science*
Stephen W. Hawking:
Black Holes & Baby Universes
A Brief History of Time

Robert Ernest Hume: *The Thirteen Principal Upanishads*
Daisaku Ikeda: *Life – An Enigma, a Precious Jewel*
Karan Singh & Daisaku Ikeda: *Humanity at the Crossroads*
Thomas à Kempis: *The Imitation of Christ*
J. Krishnamurti:
Exploration Into Insight
The First and Last Freedom
The Flight of the Eagle
Poems & Perables
The Urgency of Change
J. Krishnamurti & David Bohm: *The Ending of Time*
L. Landau and Yu. Rumer: *What is the Theory of Relativity*
Swami Madhavananda: *Viveka Chudamani of Shankracharya*
Juan Mascaro: *The Bhagwat Gita*
William H. McNeill: *Arnold J. Toynbee – A Life*
Guy Murchie:
Music of the Spheres Vol. I & II
The Seven Mysteries of Life
Nisargadatta Maharaj: *I Am That*
J. C. Palkinghorne: *The Quantum World*
A. Parthasarthy: *Vedanta Treatise*
Roger Penrose: *Shadows of the Mind*
A. O. Prickard: *Longinus on the Sublime*
S. Radhakrishnan:
The Hindu View of Life
The Bhagwat Gita
Sri Ramakrishna: *The Gospel of Sri Ramakrishna*
Swami Rama Tirtha: *In Woods of God Realization* (4 Volumes)
I. A. Richards: *Science and Poetry*
Rudy Rucker: *Infinity & The Mind*
Bertrand Russell:
New Hopes for a Changing World
ABC of Relativity
Michael Talbot: *Beyond The Quantum World*
Arnold Toynbee, Arthur Koestler & Others: *Life After Death*
Swami Vivekananda: *Complete Works* (7 Volumes)
Gary Zukav: *The Dancing Wu Li Masters*

INDEX